# PRESENT
# for SUCCESS

### A POWERFUL APPROACH
### TO BUILDING CONFIDENCE, DEVELOPING IMPACT
### AND TRANSFORMING YOUR PRESENTATIONS

**ST Training Solutions**
Success Skills Series

# ALISON LESTER

# PRESENT for SUCCESS

## A POWERFUL APPROACH TO BUILDING CONFIDENCE, DEVELOPING IMPACT AND TRANSFORMING YOUR PRESENTATIONS

**Marshall Cavendish**
Business

© 2009 Marshall Cavendish International (Asia) Private Limited
© text Alison Lester
© series title Shirley Taylor
Illustrations by Edwin Ng
Cover art by Opal Works Co. Limited

Published by Marshall Cavendish Business
An imprint of Marshall Cavendish International
1 New Industrial Road, Singapore 536196

Other Marshall Cavendish Offices
Marshall Cavendish Ltd. 5th Floor 32–38 Saffron Hill, London EC1N 8FH · Marshall Cavendish Corporation. 99 White Plains Road, Tarrytown NY 10591-9001, USA · Marshall Cavendish International (Thailand) Co Ltd. 253 Asoke, 12th Flr, Sukhumvit 21 Road, Klongtoey Nua, Wattana, Bangkok 10110, Thailand · Marshall Cavendish (Malaysia) Sdn Bhd, Times Subang, Lot 46, Subang Hi-Tech Industrial Park, Batu Tiga, 40000 Shah Alam, Selangor Darul Ehsan, Malaysia

Marshall Cavendish is a trademark of Times Publishing Limited

National Library Board Singapore Cataloguing in Publication Data

Lester, Alison Jean.
    Present for success : a powerful approach to building confidence, developing impact
        and transforming your presentations / by Alison Lester. – Singapore : Marshall
        Cavendish Business, c2009.
    p. cm. – (Success skills series)
    ISBN-13 : 978-981-261-674-6 (pbk.)
    ISBN-10 : 981-261-674-8 (pbk.)
    1. Business presentations. 2. Public speaking. I. Title. II. Series: Success skills series
    (ST Training Solutions)

HF5718.22
658.452 — dc22          · OCN311703214

Printed in Singapore by Times Graphics Pte Ltd

# PREFACE

Congratulations on picking up this copy of *Present for Success* by Alison Lester. I'm very proud that this is one of the first books in the ST Training Solutions Success Skills series. This series includes several short, practical books on a range of topics that will help you develop your skills and enhance your success at work and in your personal life.

The Success Skills series was originally created to meet the needs of participants of ST Training Solutions public workshops. After attending our workshops, many participants expressed a real desire to continue learning, to find out more about the topic, and to take it to another level. They were hungry for knowledge; just the effect I had hoped for when I set up ST Training Solutions Pte Ltd in 2007. With the Success Skills series of books, the experience and expertise of our trainers can be enjoyed by many more people.

As series editor, I've enjoyed working with the authors to make sure the books are easy-to-read, highly practical, and written in straightforward, simple language. Every book is packed with essential tools and strategies that will make you more effective and successful. We've included illustrations that reinforce some key points, because I believe we learn more if we add some fun and humour. You'll also notice some key features that highlight important learning points:

**Myth Buster**

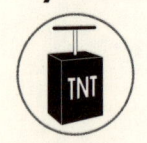

Here you will find a statement that is not true, with notes on the true facts of the matter.

**Fast Fact**

Useful snippets of information or special points to remember.

**Aha! Moment**

This is a 'light bulb' moment, when we note something you may be able to conclude from a discussion. Don't forget to note your own 'Aha! Moments' perhaps when you receive some extra insight that clarifies an important point.

**Try This**

Here you'll find a suggestion for how you can put a special point into practice, either at home or at work.

**Danger Zone**

You'll find some words of warning here, such as things to avoid or precautions to take.

**Star Tip**

At the end of each chapter you'll find a list of Star Tips — important notes to remind you about the key points.

By picking up this book you have already shown a desire to learn more. The solid advice and practical guidelines provided in this book will show you how you can really go from good to great!

Good luck!

*Shirley Taylor.*

Shirley Taylor
*Series Editor*
CEO, ST Training Solutions Pte Ltd

 **ST Training Solutions**

www.shirleytaylortraining.com
www.shirleytaylor.com

# CONTENTS

# INTRODUCTION

I've always been encouraged that a journey of a thousand miles begins with a single step, and I'm so glad that your journey to presentation excellence begins with this book.

I also want you to know that it is an interesting journey, and an entertaining journey, and that while there will certainly be comfortable places to stop and rest along the way, you will always benefit from picking up again and challenging yourself to go further.

Beyond this, it's a journey essential to your professional success. Companies are stepping up their efforts to do more with less. This means that the ability to organise and discuss information in an engaging way — a way that stimulates thought and motivates people to act — will increase your value to any organisation, as well as your sense of personal effectiveness. If you can be the one who shows a willingness to present, and to improve your presentation skills, you'll be writing yourself a ticket to a bright and interesting future. It will be a pleasure to be your guide along the way.

My own presentation career began when I worked as a tour guide at the U.S. Capitol Building when attending college. I didn't have to develop the content myself, but I did have to deliver it in a way that made my tour groups want to follow me around that big building. I also had to make sure that my groups could hear me over the handful of other guides working each room.

It wasn't until I decided to try my hand at stand-up comedy that I had to confront the questions of content, structure, pacing... and terror. Developing a stand-up monologue was perfect for forcing me to consider how best to engage an audience at the outset, how to link the various subjects in each monologue, and how to wrap things up in a memorable way. And while I'll never forget the horror of the moments when I felt so nervous that my mind went completely blank and I could hear waves crashing in my ear drums, I am grateful that they motivated me to develop strategies for calming myself and maintaining access to my brain under pressure.

Once I began working as a corporate communication trainer, I took on the challenge of developing slides to support my content. I discovered that just like structure and delivery, audiovisuals require a lot of attention, with the added aspect that they need to be updated regularly. I also learned that they can hurt us as much as they can help.

Everything I've learned along the way, from teenage tour guide to international speaker, will find a place in this book. As you start your own journey to present for success, I hope you will find the tools I describe and the advice I offer to be useful and fun.

Let's get started!


Alison Lester
www.ajlestercommunication.com

ASSESS YOURSELF

**What is your current understanding of presentation skills?**

**1. Why do I feel so nervous when I have to give a presentation?**

a) Because listeners are there to judge me.

b) Because humans are instinctively programmed to feel threatened when stared at.

c) Because I don't know what to do with my hands.

**2. When choosing which words to use to deliver my message, I need to:**

a) Avoid jargon.

b) Understand my audience so that I use words they will understand.

c) Add energy by using active rather than passive verbs.

d) Think of images that represent my message.

e) All of the above.

**3. I need to think about the impact of my voice on my listeners because:**

a) My voice can make my message more memorable.

b) I have to be careful not to strain it.

c) Vocal variety will maintain my listeners' interest for longer.

d) a and b

e) a and c

**4. A great way to deal with suddenly being unable to use my slides at a presentation is:**

a)  Practicing without my slides.

b)  Closing the meeting immediately and rescheduling.

c)  Insisting on better technical support.

d)  Crying.

**5. Which of the following things can be adjusted to improve the environment in a meeting room?**

a)  The air conditioning

b)  The seating arrangement

c)  The curtains or blinds

d)  The lighting

e)  The placement of wires

f)  a and c

g)  a through e

h)  c, d, and e

**6. If I don't pay attention to my facial expressions:**

a)  My face might not be expressing what my words are saying.

b)  I feel safer in front of a crowd.

c)  I can avoid getting deep wrinkles.

d)  My listeners are less likely to find me ugly.

**7. An appropriate way to begin developing a presentation is to:**

a) Do an Internet search on the subject.

b) Start plugging information into the corporate template.

c) Find the right pictures to go with my ideas.

d) Let my mind wander and write down everything I can think of about it.

**8. If I load my slides with information, I will:**

a) Make my message very clear to my listeners.

b) Impress the audience with my thoroughness.

c) Have to work very hard to show my listeners where to look on the slide when I am talking.

d) Remember everything I need to say.

**9. In a technical presentation, the number of slides determines the length of the presentation.**

a) True

b) False

**10. When I don't know what to do with my hands it's okay to:**

a) Put them in my pockets and jangle my change.

b) Run them continually through my hair.

c) Fiddle with my rings.

d) None of the above.

e) All of the above.

**Check out these answers to see how you fared.**

1. While (a) and (c) may seem to be the case, the reason we feel these ways lies in our basic instincts, so the answer is (b). Chapter 1 will give you lots more information on nerves, and strategies for calming them.

2. If you answered (e), you already know that using a variety of verbal choices to grab and maintain your listeners' attention is important. More on this in Chapter 3.

3. The correct answer is again (e). Not only verbal but also vocal variety is important in presenting. Try out the fun speaking exercises in Chapter 4.

4. Maybe you wanted to answer (d)! You'll learn about the importance of (b) in Chapter 1, and lots of other ways to avoid and manage trouble in Chapter 10.

5. All sorts of adjustments can improve your presentation environment, so I vote for (g). Chapter 9 discusses all these options, and more, in depth.

6. If our faces aren't convincing, our presentation message is in danger. The answer that will benefit you is (a). All of Chapter 5 is devoted to helping with this.

7. Different things work for different people. Check out Chapter 2 to understand why I feel (d) is an extremely productive first step.

8. The only guaranteed answer to this one is (c). To make your data-heavy presentations easier, take a look at Chapters 7 and 8.

9. Lots of people think this, but everything depends on how complicated the slides are. So the answer is (a). Chapter 8 goes into this as well.

10. Listeners know they can look at our hands to judge how nervous we are, so the answer is (d). Study Chapter 6 for advice on managing your body under stress.

# NERVES

**1**

*"Every little yielding to anxiety is a step away from the natural heart of man."*

Japanese proverb

## Managing stage fright so it doesn't manage you

It may well be that you're reading this book because you are interested in the question of structure, or in developing your audience engagement, but it's statistically likely that you also have a problem with stage fright. Most people do.

You'll notice that I said it's likely you have "a problem with stage fright" rather than it's likely you have stage fright. Stage fright is a fact of life for most human beings. We simply don't like to be stared at by large groups of people. Those of us who go ahead and present with enthusiasm anyway don't necessarily experience an absence of stage fright; we just no longer have a problem with it. We know it's unlikely to go away, so we work with it, finding strategies for managing it, rather than letting it control how we behave.

The reason we feel nervous under pressure, and the reason this feeling is so hard to overcome, is that it is one of our most basic instincts, and it is designed to save our lives. You don't want to eliminate this response from your system, but you do want it to occur in ways that can help your performance rather than damage it.

 **Fast Fact**

Not liking being stared at is part of the human condition.

## The physiology of fear

Let's look at what happens when we're nervous. Most humans will agree that they experience some or all of the following physical reactions:

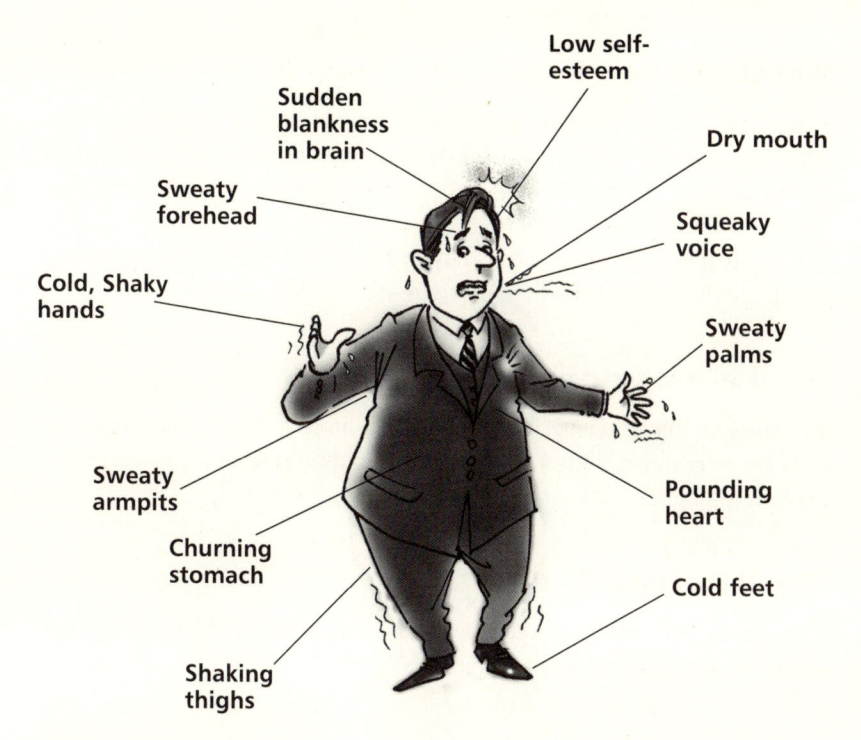

We hate when these feelings overtake us, and we're often sure that we experience them more than anyone else. But the moment that you bring up the subject you'll find that people all over the world are struggling with them too, every day. Once you come to understand their purpose, you'll begin to appreciate them more. And once you understand them, you can work on managing them.

## The power of adrenalin

Our instincts were formed in our very distant ancestors because they constantly faced physical threats, and didn't have much but their own bodies with which to do so. They evolved in a way that enabled them to produce powerful rushes of adrenalin when they felt threatened. Each adrenalin rush would set off a cascade of physical reactions designed to save them.

## Why do we shake?

We shake so much when we are nervous or scared because of the adrenalin running through our muscles, making it possible for us to fight or to flee. When your legs are full of adrenalin, you can run very, very fast. When you don't run, the adrenalin doesn't get used up, and you shake. The same goes for your hands. They're ready to fight, but if you're only using them to point at a flipchart or screen, they'll shake too.

## Why does my heart pound?

It's easier to run when our heart rate is up. In fact, deep breathing isn't possible in a sprint. It's not efficient. So our heart gets ready for the mad dash or the attack, and we start to breathe very shallowly.

## Why do I get sweaty?

If our hands and arms and head are wet with sweat, it's going to be much easier to slip out of an enemy's grasp, isn't it?

## Why does my voice squeak?

Adrenalin also has an awkward effect on our voices. Back when we were up against mountain lions or angry tribes, it didn't matter. We didn't start trying to talk things through until much later in our evolution.

## What causes cold hands and feet?

If our blood stops flowing so strongly to our hands and feet, making them grow cold, we are much less likely to bleed to death if we're wounded there. Also, limiting blood flow to our outer layer of muscle and focusing it into our core makes these outer muscles tougher, and better at fending off blows.

## Why does my tummy suffer?

Sometimes our bowels are so affected by the rush of adrenalin that we need to move them, and must find a toilet immediately. Even this is designed to save us. When you perceive a high level of threat and your heart rate rises to 175 beats per minute and above, your body starts shutting down 'non-essential' activity like intestinal control. You'll be grateful for this if you're ever running away from an angry animal and soil yourself. Animals don't like to eat smelly meat.

## Why does my brain go blank?

How can a blank brain possibly be designed to save our lives? We often feel that it will do just the opposite. Think about this: The brain is so analytical that if there weren't a mechanism to stop it from trying to figure out the viability of each possible escape route, it would still be doing the equations as the attacking animal sank its fangs into our neck. Adrenalin shuts off the analytical function of the brain, and allows for only one thought: Fight or flight? Fight or flight? Fight or flight?

## Why does my self-esteem suffer?

High levels of adrenalin stop the production of serotonin in the brain. Serotonin is the chemical that gives us our sense of well-being. The beautiful idea behind this is that if our brain can make us feel as awful as possible about having been in a threatening situation, and as awful as possible about ourselves and our ability to manage such situations, it can make us avoid them completely in the future.

For all these reasons, we prefer to avoid presenting. We feel we are under threat, and we feel physically, mentally, and emotionally miserable. The key, then, is to change our perception that we are under threat.

 **Aha! Moment**

When I feel awful at the prospect of a presentation, it is a perfectly natural response, and doesn't mean there's anything wrong with me.

## Changing fear to fun, mentally and physically

When our most basic instincts are shouting at us, telling us that if we are being stared at by a group of people it could be that they are about to reject us, we need to get our higher functions to shout something back. We need to turn up the volume on our reality channel. There are a few great ways to do so.

### 1.  Positive self-talk

The first method is mental. We need to change how we talk to ourselves under pressure, motivating rather than discouraging ourselves. Take a look at these examples:

| Instead of | Tell yourself |
|---|---|
| "It's so awful to be in front of people who are judging my every word." | "I'm here to gain from the experience of sharing information with other interested people. Cool!" |
| "I've never met any of these people. How can I possibly win them over?" | "It will be good to greet people as they come in, shake a few hands, and start some new relationships. I'm sure we can benefit from knowing each other." |
| "No one's showing any response. I must be so boring." | "Just because I can't tell what they're thinking doesn't mean they hate me. I'll ask some questions to engage the crowd." |

 **Aha! Moment**

For every negative "What if?" there is a positive alternative. "What if this presentation goes as badly as last week's?" will become "What if I use what I learned from last week and make some great improvements?"

## 2. Find a personal strategy

Sometimes it takes some real internal shouting to turn a situation around. I speak from painful experience.

I was invited to sing as a guest performer in a concert by a very talented and charming quartet of musicians. When the concert began, I was seated in the audience. The idea was that we were going to make it look like I was an audience member with something to say, and then when they invited me up to talk, I would burst into song. So I sat in my seat, watching the three other singers perform their fabulous first numbers. I felt my heart pounding as if it were in my throat. My hands were freezing. And other than the first half of the first line, the song had completely left my head.

I heard screaming in my brain, "Oh no! Oh no! Oh no! I can't remember the words!" Naturally, the more I panicked, the more adrenalin went rushing through my body. I realised I needed to practice what I preach, so I turned up the volume on the reality channel, and talked back to myself. "I've known this song since I was fifteen years old," my rational self told my nervous self. "I sang it perfectly less than an hour ago." My heart was still trying to climb out of my body, and the moment I stopped speaking to myself rationally the screaming started again. I tried to remember the words to the song but I couldn't. And all the while the moment when I would have to walk on stage drew nearer and nearer.

There was nothing else to do but stop thinking about the song and get firm. So I began repeating a mantra: "I know the words to this song. I know the words to this song. I know the words to this song. I know the words to this song." I repeated it over and over in my head, allowing no other thoughts to make their way to the surface, knowing that if they did I'd have another adrenalin rush and would feel even worse.

"I know the words to this song," I repeated firmly to myself as the third singer began asking questions of the audience, which was my cue to start getting involved. I repeated it as I walked toward the stage. I repeated it, smiling warmly at the crowd of 250 listeners, as I took my place behind the microphone and nodded to the pianist to begin playing, and I repeated it again right up until the moment when I opened my mouth to sing.

The song poured out of my mouth, completely intact. I just had to get out of its way.

So for me, a mantra was the key. For a friend of mine, it's a shared laugh. Whenever he has a meeting that he feels stressed about on his agenda, he makes a point of spending some time beforehand with a colleague who has a wonderful sense of humour. He knows that when he comes out of this colleague's office, he'll be smiling and feeling more relaxed. He brings this smile into the meeting with him, and it helps him keep a positive attitude about the task at hand.

 **Myth Buster**

You can stay calm by preparing right up until the moment you have to present.

Wrong! Doing this often has the opposite effect. If you are rehearsing in the car on the way to the meeting, in the elevator on the way up to the meeting, and in the reception area before the meeting, you are telling yourself that you are not ready. Listen to music, read a magazine, allow your brain to relax and avoid an adrenalin rush. Tell yourself you'll be fine, and it's more likely that you will.

## 3. Call it what you will: cognitive reframing

It can help enormously to remove the word 'nervous' from your discussions of presenting. This will help you to avoid what's called 'the second wave of fear'. When we feel threatened, we have a rush of adrenalin, and then, when we are horrified that we feel threatened ("Oh no! I feel nervous! This is terrible!") we set off another rush of adrenalin. It's important to interrupt this vicious cycle.

A great way to do this is to stop thinking of yourself as nervous and start thinking of yourself as thrilled. When we're excited, our hearts beat faster, our mouths go dry, and we shake a bit as well. It's the same physical condition, and yet we don't hate it. On the contrary, we seek the feeling out! If you start thinking of yourself as thrilled by the opportunity to speak, you are less likely to suffer from adrenalin overload, and will broadcast a much more positive energy to your listeners.

## 4. Let's get physical

Another way to combat the discomfort of presentation nerves is to use the adrenalin that is causing it. This means performing physical activities that help drain the chemical out of your system. You can, for example:

- Walk around the outside of the building, the block, or the parking lot.
- Walk up and down several flights of stairs.
- Do jumping jacks or squat thrusts.
- Roll a newspaper or magazine into a tube, go into the washroom, and battle it out with the toilet. I know someone who does this, and it really helps him go into his presentation without the nervous aggression that adrenalin pumps into his system!

Any of these activities will not only use up some of the adrenalin you feel pumping in your muscles, but will also give you a nice rosy glow. Remember to wipe down your forehead, tidy your hair, and tuck in your shirt before the presentation starts, though!

What if there's no opportunity to do these things before your talk? What if you're listening to other speakers, and you can't or don't want to leave the room? There are several things you can do:

- Clench your thigh and buttock muscles as you sit, and do so for as long as you can. Take a break, and do it again. This will use up adrenalin and make you feel stronger.

- Practice deep breathing. Bring your heart rate down, and your brain will get the message that you're relaxed.

- Smile. Smiling also tells your brain that you're actually doing fine, and you can feel the effect on your body right away. Plus, you look nicer!

- Focus your concentration on what's happening in the room. Listen carefully to the speaker, so you can refer to what he or she has said in your own talk, adding value to your participation.

Once you're on your feet in front of the two, or twenty, or two hundred people you're speaking to, you can't do jumping jacks (well, you can, with repercussions) but you can continue your deep breathing as you pause during your speech. I also find it extremely helpful to stand with my feet flat on the floor and clench my thigh and buttock muscles as tight as I can for as long as I can. It has an immediately calming effect on me.

### Try This

Stand up with your feet about hip-width apart. Clench your thigh and buttock muscles tightly. Make sure that the tension in your legs doesn't travel up into your torso. Keep your upper body and arms relaxed. Keep clenching. Be aware of how nicely planted you feel, and how secure. Because your legs are strong and stable, the top of your body can let go a bit.

This is a very nice way to start a presentation. You'll feel confident. When you've clenched as long as you can, go ahead and release your legs, and perhaps move a bit in the space. If you feel your adrenalin levels rise again, find another good place to stand, plant yourself like a tall, strong tree, and keep delivering your message with clarity and power.

 **Star Tips for managing presentation nerves**

1. Remember that stage fright is a natural, basic instinct.

2. Change how you talk to yourself under pressure, from negative to positive.

3. Don't over-prepare as it can make you as nervous as not preparing enough.

4. Reframe your perspective so that you see yourself as excited to be presenting rather than nervous about it.

5. Engage in physical activity to reduce adrenalin levels and keep your brain functioning smoothly under pressure.

6. Smile!

# DEVELOPING YOUR CONTENT, DEVELOPING YOUR STRUCTURE

*"A picture, it is said, is worth a thousand words, but cannot a few well-spoken words convey as many pictures?"*

Author Unknown

2

## The first step

Okay, now that you've had my pep talk on managing your nerves, we can dig in to the nitty-gritty of putting together a solid, relevant, interesting and motivating presentation.

The first step is to forget all about your presentation.

I'm serious. Thinking about your presentation too early in the game will limit your content. Think instead about your *subject*. You probably won't need everything you know about your subject for your presentation, but it is very important for your sense of confidence that you lay out as much as you can on the subject before you start designing your presentation.

## Getting your ideas to flow

### Mind Maps (or brain webs)

The best way I have discovered for getting the ideas to flow is to use a tool like a Mind Map, or a brain web (see Illustration 2.1). Such techniques have also been referred to as tornado diagramming, balloon diagramming, concept mapping, and think-linking. Unlike outlines or lists, these tools allow you to set all your ideas down in a way that gives them equal importance. They also allow your ideas to flow in many directions, whereas outlines limit your mind to a strict structure. It's dangerous to get into structure too early, as you might well miss out on a very juicy area of discussion.

There are lots of resources on the Internet and in bookstores, particularly on Mind Mapping, but the basic concept involves beginning with your central subject in the middle of a blank piece of paper, and allowing all relevant associations with this subject to flow out of your mind. You write them down on the page, radiating out from the centre. The more associations you can make, and the more deeply you investigate each of these associations (so that each association with the central subject has its own sub-associations coming off it like branches), the richer a body of information you have to draw from and the more interesting the links you will be able to make.

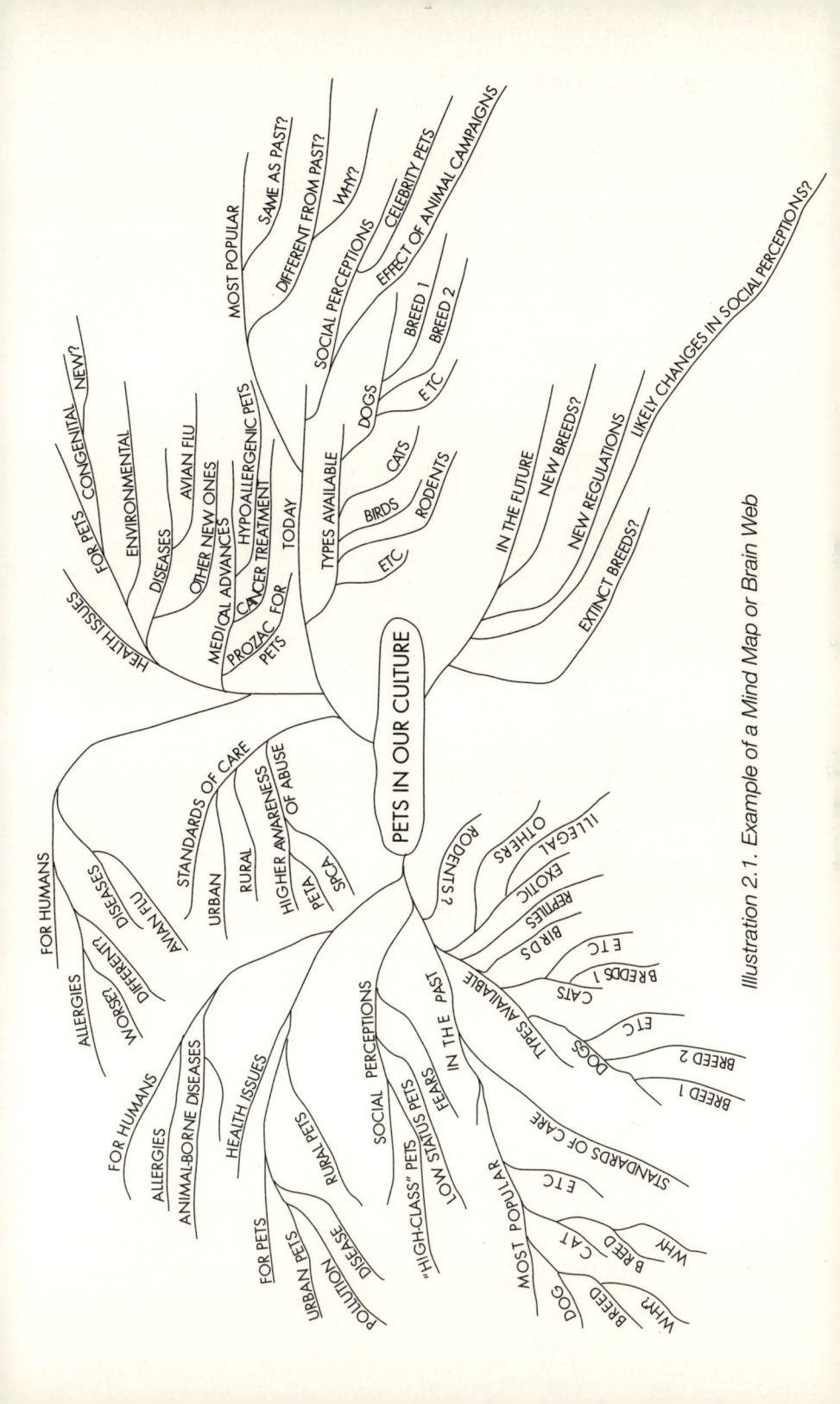

*Illustration 2.1. Example of a Mind Map or Brain Web*

As you can see, every one of the arteries branching off from the centre has sub-arteries, and each of these can be developed even further. It's exciting to see how deeply you can get into a subject just by asking your brain a few questions and letting it make all its natural connections.

## Free association

Another way to get as many ideas out as possible is just by free association. Take a piece of blank paper and write down anything and everything you can think of to do with your subject, any way that works for you. Don't try to organise the thoughts, just write them down. As with the other tools, leave no stone unturned, and censor no ideas. To do this, it certainly helps to consider questions such as these:

- What are the cons of this subject, as well as the pros?
- How has this subject changed over time?
- How are things likely to look in the future?
- Do men and women look at this subject differently?
- Is there a difference in attitudes between generations?
- What is my personal experience of this subject?
- What are the dangers associated with this subject?

Some of these questions may not be immediately relevant to your subject, but keep them in mind for other subjects as well. You need to be as inclusive as possible in your thinking. If you've thought about all sides of an issue, you will be better prepared when it comes time for questions.

 **Aha! Moment**

When I allow my brain to think what it wants, as opposed to telling it what to think, I can surprise myself with the extent of the associations I can make.

**Try This**

> Choose a topic relevant to you and, using a Mind Map or free association, write down anything and everything you can think of to do with your subject, in any way that works for you. Don't try to organise the thoughts, just write them down. Allow your ideas to flow and don't censor anything. Just let your brain start working and see how it feels. Take your time.

## Plugging in to the World Wide Web

Once you have investigated the wealth of information in your brain for associations on your subject, get online.

Why didn't I say get online first? This goes back to the question of confidence. Show yourself what you know first. If you take time over this, you'll be surprised at how much is already in your head. You'll feel good about what you've been able to produce on the spot. When you feel you're scraping the bottom of the barrel, it then helps a great deal to share your thoughts with a colleague or friend. They will have their own ideas, and may be able to point out something missing on your map of associations that will open up another area of thought for you. You can do the same for them when they are preparing their information too.

*Then* go online. Having gone through the association step first, you will be able to do a much more focused online search on the many facets of your subject. You'll find stories and statistics to back up your ideas, and you'll uncover new areas to develop thoughts on.

## Who's listening?

Now that you've laid out all the information you can develop on the subject, start thinking about the audience who will listen to your presentation.

| | |
|---|---|
| **Who are they?** | Are they clients? |
| | Is it your boss? |
| | Is it your team? |
| | Are they people in your industry, such as an audience at a conference? |
| | |
| **What is the audience like?** | Do they tend to be negative? |
| | Do they ask a lot of questions? |
| | Are they at your level in the hierarchy, or higher, or lower? |
| | |
| **What is your objective?** | Are you merely sharing information? |
| | Are you trying to convince them to buy a product? |
| | Are you warning them off a strategy? |

Only when you have answered these questions about your objective and your listeners does it really make any sense at all to start choosing the information you will use to achieve your goals.

Take a look at your associations now. With your objective and your audience firmly in mind, start choosing your content.

 **Myth Buster**

As long as I'm clear on my own objective, I can be convincing.

Sorry! Unless you understand the objective or objectives of your audience you won't be able to really connect with them and steer their perspective the way you want it to go.

## Putting it all together

Let's say for example that you are an industry analyst and your subject is mobile phones. You've done a Mind Map that includes information on the development of mobile phones; historical trends in mobile phone usage, current trends, and what's ahead; changes in the technology; changes in the design; the differences between men's and women's tastes in phones; regional differences in demand and supply; the major competitors; the question of waste and recycling; the differences in successful and unsuccessful marketing strategies; and more.

For one client, you may have conducted a presentation on current trends that included a discussion of differences in regional requirements and differences in men's and women's tastes in different countries. This time, however, you will be speaking at a conference about production-related issues. Your audience will be made up of people involved in production themselves.

Analyse your audience. First of all, you know that you will be able to speak at a pretty sophisticated level, and use a lot of their jargon without being misunderstood. Secondly, you know that they will not be interested in what's already happened, but rather in what the future may hold. They'll probably want your thoughts on how to get ahead of the coming wave. They will no doubt want statistics, but like most people they will also want to be engaged with real-life stories, above all those that mirror their own concerns.

Now look at your material and pull out what suits your audience's needs and expectations. It would make perfect sense to talk about trends in customer demand and taste while linking this with trends in technological development and new materials. Do you have any stories of manufacturers who have experimented with new materials? What has worked? What else might work? Given current consumer concerns with the environment, what can you recommend to the manufacturer in terms of materials and recycling that hasn't yet been done?

**Danger Zone**

Insufficient attention to who your audience is can mean your presentation turns out to be a waste of time, both for them and for you.

## The many ways to give life to your structure

Once you've understood your audience and pulled out the relevant content from all your materials, you can start thinking about how to structure it for maximum clarity and impact.

Unfortunately, when some people start thinking about the structure of their presentation, all the life goes out of it. They know their presentation needs an opening, a body including a number of relevant points, and a closing. That's good; it does. But too often they ignore the following facts:

- The opening is an opportunity to truly interest and engage the audience and lay the groundwork for what's to come.

- The points in the body of the presentation will really shine if they employ tools for linking them both to their main point and to each other in clear and memorable ways.

- The closing provides a platform for a call to action.

**Myth Buster**

When trainers tell you to "Tell them what you're going to tell them, tell them, then tell them what you told them," that's all they mean.

It's not. That would be too boring. What they mean is, maintain a solid, logical structure that links all your points. Stay clear and coherent. And when you tell them what you told them, do it in a way that takes the subject to the next level.

You might want to think of your structure in terms of a gymnastics floor routine. A gymnast will design her routine to open in a way that both impresses and engages you. She will pepper the middle of the routine with high points that are remarkable in their own way, but will make sure they are absolutely relevant to what she is trying to display and in line with mood of the rest of the routine. Then she will finish with a bang.

If she opens big, and closes big, but the middle of the routine is entirely forgettable, she will not come across as dependable. You might even get so bored that you start watching something else and miss her closing completely.

A lot of people work very hard on the openings and the closings of their presentations, and hope that the middle works out somehow. Other people do a great job with the opening and the middle, but don't pay attention to developing a truly motivating ending. Some people start off badly and pick up steam, ending just fine, but will have lost some of their audience along the way.

**Fast Fact**

A solid structure isn't enough. What's important is what you do with it.

## The keys to being memorable

To deliver a memorable presentation, you must be able to show how all your points relate to your main objective as well as how they link to each other. The key to succeeding in this lies in developing appropriate and engaging transitions. These transitions will make the structure of your presentation obvious.

There are as many examples of how to do this as there are creative presenters on the planet, but I'll describe a handful of very different ways to give you an idea of some of your options.

### 1. Looking back, looking ahead

In this type of presentation, you will break the body down into three sections: past, present, and future. People love to be taken chronologically through time if the story is worth the journey. Let's say it's your job to give a year-end speech about your company's direction. You might work out your structure like this:

- Introduction: In this short talk, I'll be taking you on a walk through the company's history in order to look into the future.

- Point 1: The company's early days were tough, but we persevered and innovated. (Describe)

- Transition: Is it any wonder then that we have such a strong standing in the market today?

- Point 2: Our standing is nice and solid in several areas, but there are currently some trends that we need to develop a response to. (Describe)

- Transition: Recent technological developments do pose what some might call a threat, but we can easily see this as an opportunity.

- Point 3: Our strategy for the future shows us capitalising on this new technology, not shying away from it. (Describe)

- Closing: I look forward to having you join me in the next stage of this exciting journey.

## 2.  Fairytale analogy

What if, for example, you are a doctor, and are going to explain a disease and its treatment to a group of children? In this case, you might choose to lay it out like this:

- Introduction: What are the elements of a good story? An interesting situation? A villain? A hero? A happy ending? Well, my story today has all these things.

- Point 1: So what's going on when our story begins? (Describe the situation.)

- Transition: We all love a good villain, don't we?

- Point 2: Who's the villain in this story? (Describe the disease, and what it's doing.)

- Transition: If we only had a villain this story would be a tragedy, so we need a good hero too.

- Point 3: Who's the hero? (Describe the treatment, and how it arrived on the scene.)

- Transition: Now we have a villain and a hero. What happens next?

- Point 4: We have a battle! (Describe how the hero resolves the situation by vanquishing the villain.)

- Closing: Now you can see how much your new knowledge of the illness and the treatment will help you all to be heroes too.

In fact, this type of set-up doesn't only work with children. Adults find it entertaining as well! It can be a nice surprise if you are expecting a very dry, technical presentation, and instead you are taken into a fairytale, and you come out with all the relevant information nonetheless.

## 3.  A variety of other examples

Here are some more examples of structure with very natural transitions:

- Lay out the players in a certain situation as if they were animals, and identify their distinguishing characteristics. Which one is the lion, dominating the terrain? Which one is a gazelle, trying to keep out of trouble, easily startled by any change? Call to action: Underline the importance of being a good park ranger.

- Liken the steps of a project to the stages of a mountain climb. Establish what needs to be done as preparation, at base camp, further up in more treacherous territory, and at the summit. Call to action: Make sure everyone involved has a common understanding and common values so they communicate well along the way and enjoy the adventure.

- Compare different market players with well-known athletes. Call to action: When dealing with these players, make sure to bring a racket if tennis is their game, or clubs if they have more of a golfer's temperament.

- Discuss your own learning process early in your career, and describe how you are applying this anew in a changing financial environment. Call to action: I hope you will join me in learning as much as we can, and in sharing this learning every day, since it is the learners who will get ahead in this market.

Now that you see some of the interesting approaches that successful presenters use for their structure, I'm sure your mind will start recognising many more options.

 **Aha! Moment**

The sky's the limit when it comes to options for packaging my information. Coming up with interesting ways to do so makes presenting more fun for me, and more memorable for my listeners.

Have fun with it!

## Star Tips for developing your content and structure

1. Don't think about your presentation too early in the process, or this will limit your content.

2. Add richness to your information by using tools such as Mind Maps to develop ideas and associations.

3. Consider your audience before you begin structuring your content.

4. Don't ruin your opening with a boring agenda. Your opening is an opportunity to truly interest and engage the audience.

5. Make your presentation memorable by linking all points to the main objective, as well as showing the links between these points.

6. Be creative in the ways you give life to your presentation structure.

# TOOLS FOR DELIVERY — YOUR WORDS

*"I would never use a long word where a short one would answer the purpose. I know there are professors in this country who 'ligate' arteries. Other surgeons only tie them, and it stops the bleeding just as well."*

Oliver Wendell Holmes

## Managing audience attention

A simple rule of thumb goes like this: Under the best conditions, a human being will concentrate on what another human being is saying for as many minutes as their age. So a one-year-old will listen for a minute, a five-year-old for five, a 15-year-old for 15, and so on up to the age of 20. After that, it levels off. As a result, it's much too much to expect a group of adults to listen attentively for more than a 20-minute stretch. This doesn't bode well when we have to give two-hour presentations!

What you do with your voice, your face, and your body will have a huge impact on how well people to listen to you, but we will address these areas in the coming chapters. In this chapter, we're concentrating on how you choose what to say rather than how to say it. So while you must not expect the words to speak for themselves without added emphasis, choosing good words and powerful images will certainly help the message.

It makes no sense to develop a presentation that isn't clear and relevant. It also makes no sense to develop a presentation that is so simple it leaves no mark on the listener. The trick, then, is to come up with a blend of style and substance that is meaningful for you and appropriate for your audience. Much of the style and substance will come from how you choose which points to make and which structural tools you use to deliver them. Much will also come from the individual words you say.

## Keep it simple, with impact

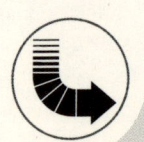 **Fast Fact**

Humans have not only limited time, but also a limited attention span. You need to respect this by keeping your presentations simple and engaging.

Contrast these two sentences:

**#1**     *"Unfortunately, our organisation has not been able to manage the disparity between its output and the demands on its financial base."*

**#2**     *"We're broke."*

While the second sentence contains only two syllables, it has many times the emotional power of the first. It comes straight to the point, and doesn't hide behind difficult terms. Now, if your goal in your presentation is to pull the wool over your listeners' eyes, then by all means go overboard with the vocabulary. But if your objective is to be clear, interesting and motivating, stick to words we all understand, and keep your sentences relatively short.

## The well-placed "zinger"

While you are sticking to punchy, powerful words and manageable, coherent sentences, it's a nice touch to throw in great descriptive words that really capture the imagination from time to time. This is especially true if you like to use stories in your presentations. To see what I mean, read through these two examples and see if they feel different to you.

**Story 1**     *"I have a client who was very nervous about his company's prospects. He was regularly losing staff, and he was concerned that he couldn't keep up with the competition."*

**Story 2**     *"I have a client who was desperate about his company's prospects. Staff were leaving in droves, and he felt like easy prey for the competition."*

In the first example, the words are simpler, but the message takes longer. It's clear, but a bit dull. Most audiences will feel concern, but not very deeply. In the second example, more descriptive words are used to intensify the feeling, and the image of feeling like prey drives it home.

The language is accessible, but also compelling due to its stronger emotional content.

## Keeping your language robust

There are several ways in which we undermine the strength of our message. Beyond a weak structure and lack of clarity of purpose, we also use words that dull our impact. Primary among these are out-of-date language, weak verbs, and passive verbs.

### *Out-of-date language*

In a misguided effort possibly to sound authoritative, some people choose language that went out of date with our grandparents. Things like this:

> *"It is my great pleasure to be in attendance at this event today. Heretofore, our organisation has had the privilege of helping to select the candidates for this award. Being on the receiving end of the reward is an honour we had never allowed ourselves to imagine. We are extremely grateful."*

While such language does indicate how seriously the speaker is taking the moment, it also indicates how seriously she takes herself, and is a lot of language to wade through for the listener. Try something like this instead:

> *"I am absolutely delighted to be here today. Until now, we've been privileged to be on the selection committee. We never imagined that we would be chosen ourselves. What a great honour. Thank you all so much."*

If you have done research on your listeners, and you know that they expect you to use a lot of complicated language, by all means do so, if you can pull it off. They might feel a lack of respect if you take a more casual approach. But these days it's much more common for listeners to appreciate a speaker's effort to be clear and engaging, as if their presentation were a conversation rather than a speech. Watch out for using dusty old language that will put a distance between you and your listeners rather than bring you together.

## Weak words

While it's important to keep our language simple, above all for those of us who speak to international audiences, it is equally important to keep our language lively. Some words are simply more powerful than others. Here are some examples:

| | |
|---|---|
| Sales rose very fast. | *Sales skyrocketed.* |
| Nothing is happening in the market. | *The market is lifeless.* |
| Our window frames have a new design and will satisfy your needs. | *Our improved window frames will amaze you.* |
| Sally was very scared. | *Sally shook like a leaf.* |

You can see how often the more lively word is one that serves as a metaphor or analogy. These words paint pictures that speaking literally just cannot.

Other weak words are those we use to sound humble, but which damage our credibility and lower our status. Try to shift toward a more definitive voice, as in these examples.

| | |
|---|---|
| I hope to be able to show you… | *I will show you…* |
| If you don't mind, I'll now discuss… | *I'm excited to be able to discuss…* |

| | |
|---|---|
| Maybe you'll be able to understand how… | *I'm sure you'll see very clearly how…* |
| In this presentation, I'll try to give you… | *This presentation offers you…* |

I know that in some contexts — for example when speaking to a very senior colleague in a very hierarchical company or country — it will benefit you to soften your language so as not to cause offence. What's important is to recognise that if you do so at all times, you may well be judged as cowardly. Understanding your audience will help you decide which words will have your desired effect.

### Danger Zone

Albert Einstein is attributed to have said that everything should be made as simple as possible, but not simpler. He was referring to science, but the same goes for presentations. Beware of simplifying them so much that you suck the life out of them.

### *Passive verbs*

Passive verbs mean that something is done to the subject of the sentence, rather than the subject being active.

**Passive:**  The investigation was concluded by the client, and the paperwork was signed.

**Active:**  The client concluded the investigation and signed the paperwork.

Can you see how, when we use the passive voice rather than the active voice, we inadvertently drain a bit of life out of our message? Consider this text:

*"Our pet food campaign was noticed by the advertising industry awards board, as it was considered to be both original and meaningful. We were asked to be part of the showcase at their annual convention, and also invited to speak on a panel. As you can imagine, we were delighted to participate, and were much enriched by the ability to share our experiences with other marketing professionals at the convention."*

Think for a bit about how you might make the verbs active. There are certainly many ways to do it. What approach would you take?

If you're not quite sure, here's one possible way:

*"Our pet food campaign caught the eye of the advertising industry awards board for its originality and its meaningfulness. As a result, they asked us not only to be part of their annual convention showcase, but also to speak on a panel. It was a great honour, and of course we said yes! The opportunity to share our experiences with other marketing professionals at the convention was priceless, and we had a truly enriching time."*

By using the active voice you've made your pet food campaign the hero of the story, rather than the awards board. Can you see how using active rather than passive language adds energy to the text?

 **Aha! Moment**

When I change my passive verbs to active verbs, I will immediately sound more dynamic.

## Jargon as a foreign language

It's wonderful how industries develop their own specific terms, acronyms, and abbreviations. However, it's important to remember that these terms are a completely foreign language to people outside the industry. Terminology might not even be consistent within an industry as different terms can be used in different countries. A British friend of mine with a financial business in Asia had a meeting with some Americans working in the same field in the United States. When they began using a term he didn't understand again and again, he didn't want to appear ignorant, so he excused himself and went into a nearby office to look up the term on the Internet! You don't want any of your listeners to feel this way, so it can be very good for your relationship to check in with them as to whether or not the terms you are using are familiar to them. And if they are from outside your industry, naturally it is best to use layman's terms instead of the very specialised language you use with your colleagues.

## What you don't say can be just as important

It's well worth the effort to spend time choosing the right words to say in a meeting or speech, but we often then muddy our message with meaningless words like "um", "you know", "mmm", "actually", "sort of" and "ok?"

All these words pop out of our mouths when we feel the need to think. Why? Because we are afraid of silence. However, it might help if you take a moment to put yourself in the position of listener. Do you mind it when a speaker pauses to think? Probably not. In fact, you likely welcome a moment to digest what's been said so far. What's more, you will have a much easier time remembering what is said if there are pauses here and there in the presentation. But as speakers, fearing rejection, we worry that taking a moment to collect our thoughts will reflect badly on us. Like anything else, it's not what you do, it's how you do it.

People who use these thinking noises and words to excess in their presentations are largely unaware of doing so. You may be one of them, but have no idea that you are. So ask! Ask your colleagues to give you feedback on how you talk and the words you use. Ask permission to set up a camera in a meeting room during a team meeting, then play it back afterwards to hear what your verbal tics are. I guarantee you will be surprised. We don't hear these thinking words as we're saying them because we hear our thoughts instead. Once you start listening for them, they will pop up like mushrooms.

**Aha! Moment**

I'll be able to start dealing with the filler words I'm using once I hear them for myself.

### Battling the urge to "um", you know

My experience of reducing how often I say "um", and helping others to do the same, has taught me that the best way to do so is simply to slow yourself down. When you speak more slowly, you will calm yourself down and you will have time to keep your thoughts organised. An added benefit I've found is that I can literally hear the "um" coming down the pipeline in my brain when I slow down, so I am more easily able to avoid saying it.

Saying "you know" too much really reduces your authority in any type of presentation. Fortunately it can be battled in the same way as "um" and "ah". Record yourself either on a voice recorder or on camera during a meeting or public speaking engagement, or have a colleague count how many times you say these things, in order to understand just how severe the problem may be. Then slow down to a pace that allows you to avoid saying the words. When you feel them coming, pause. Choose your next words at a reasonable pace. Your listeners will appreciate the effort you are making to be as clear as possible.

### The reality of "actually"

I wish I had ten cents for every time a presenter said "actually" without meaning it. The overuse of "actually" feels like a virus in some places! You end up listening to language like this: "This slide actually shows you the current market for mobile phones in Asia Pacific. We've actually been watching for signs of a downturn due to the current economy."

Maybe you're so used to hearing "actually" used like this that you're wondering where the problem lies. The word "actually" is synonymous with "in reality". Look at those two sentences again and replace "actually" with "in reality". How does it sound? It's ridiculous.

Give "actually" back its true meaning. Use it in sentences where you are contrasting an opinion with a fact: "Many people think that teenagers underestimate the dangers of smoking. Actually, when surveyed, many teenagers believed that smoking is more lethal than it is."

### Sorting out "sort of"

I recently heard a presenter say, "So that's how I sort of see our sort of plan for the pitch next week." It was clear that he used "sort of" not only as a filler word as he was thinking while he talked, but also as a way to sound humble. Think about it, though. If he's been asked to present a plan for a pitch, his team will want to hear that he has confidence in his ideas, won't they? It's confident, but not arrogant, simply to say, "So that's how I see our plan for next week's pitch."

## A picture paints a thousand words

You will need more than an intellectual connection with your listeners if you are trying to motivate them to act — to adopt your strategy, to buy your product, to employ you. You need to touch their emotions somehow. Drawing some sort of picture with your words does this very well. There are several ways to do this:

## Personal stories

Telling a relevant story about yourself is a wonderful way to get into your subject and to bring your listeners closer to you at the same time. For example, the head of a department whose objective is to motivate her team to get their accounts cleared more quickly might open with:

> *"I was at a management meeting last week where we discussed the backlog of pending accounts, and it was really scary. The number is mounting, and we're about to really start feeling the pain as a company. So today I'm going to talk to you about my strategies for dealing with this, and to assure you that we can certainly improve the situation when we work to help each other on this issue."*

You can see how she is making her objective clear while at the same time she opens up emotionally to the group, so that they know she didn't call the meeting to affix blame or to issue orders. She's in this thing together with them, and she's got ideas to help. As a result, the group is more likely to listen attentively and get on board.

Depending on the situation, it can be appropriate for you to use quite a long story in your presentation. Some people also split them, starting their presentation with the beginning of a story, then finishing the story in the conclusion, in order to underline their points and take them a step further in a very satisfying way.

## Quotes

We often hear speakers quoting famous people in their presentations, and this can be very interesting. Sometimes, though, it feels as if the presentation was designed around the quote, rather than the quote having been chosen to support the presentation. Also, when you quote a famous person, they are not usually talking about you or your company, so there's no guarantee that the audience will feel the link.

An effective alternative is to quote someone closer to home by thinking through relevant conversations you've had with important people in your life. Have they said anything useful lately? Let's imagine you sell cat food. You could start a pitch to distributors like this:

> *"The other day my neighbour said to me, 'Your cat's fur is so nice and shiny, so healthy-looking. I've heard that feeding them raw egg can do that. Is that what you do?' I told her about the egg in our newly formulated dry food, and now all three of her cats are hooked too."*

In this way, you not only get to underline the important ingredient in your new product, but you also show that you're fully engaged in the product yourself.

## Aphorisms

An aphorism is a familiar saying, which means people will probably recognise it. That's good. But it also means that unless it relates in an interesting way to your subject, it can sound trite. For example, it's pretty dull to say that dogs are Man's best friend if you're talking about dogs. But what about this?

> *"Dogs are Man's best friend. I think we agree. So I'm looking into which canine qualities we, as a company, can adopt in order to be our customers' best friend. Here's what I've come up with."*

Rather than boring your listener with a tired old phrase, you're using it in a new way. And they're still listening.

## Analogies: similes and metaphors

In a simile, you say that two apparently unrelated things are like each other. With a metaphor, you actually say they are each other. For example, "My son eats like a vacuum cleaner" is a simile. "My assistant is an angel" is a metaphor. Both are ways of making analogies.

Analogies are wonderful for introducing verbal imagery into your presentation. I find this is particularly true if the content is quite technical and you are speaking to a less-than-tech-savvy audience. Here are a few examples:

> *"You can think of this innovation as a metronome. The software has always been playing the right notes, but now it is doing so at exactly the right time."*

*"My office is like some sort of no-man's land in the middle of a cold war. People from accounting come and talk to me, and people from design come and talk to me, but I can't seem to get them to engage with each other."*

*"We've positioned our company on the high dive. Plenty of our competitors are doing their tricks down on the springboards, but we've made it clear that our goals are higher. It's a risky position we've taken, but it offers us the chance to distinguish ourselves. What we need now is to make sure that we are in perfect shape for the dive."*

## Statistics

You can't just introduce numbers into your presentation and expect them to have impact on their own. You must choose your statistics carefully, and deliver them with emphasis. Using a striking statistic in your opening, or at the beginning of a section, can be an excellent way to get and keep audience attention. Here's one:

*"We tend to think of smoking as being on the decline. At the moment, smoking related-diseases kill one in ten adults globally, or cause four million deaths. But by 2030, if current trends continue, smoking will kill one in six people."*

## Imagination

Asking your listeners to imagine something along with you is a sure-fire way to keep their attention. It's just about impossible for human beings not to imagine what they are being asked to imagine. If I say, "Imagine a pirate ship," you see it in your mind, don't you? Your listeners will do the same. You can use the tool like this:

*"Imagine one of your staff has an irate customer on the telephone, and is beginning to get frustrated and panicky because he doesn't know how to handle the situation. He hasn't been trained. So he just says what comes to mind..."*

It's everyone's nightmare to have an employee damage business because of mishandling a phone call. By getting them to imagine the situation and feel the unhappy emotions that go along with it you can easily drive home the need for training.

## Questions

Asking questions is another tried and true way to keep your listener's mind with you, to begin relating to them, and to work some emotion into the mix.

Some presenters like to ask questions that expect a show of hands: "How many of you have ever struggled through a leveraged buyout?" If people actually do raise their hands, you'll benefit from having an idea of how knowledgeable your audience is. You'll also be able to follow your question with something like, "Well, those of you who have will know how painful it can be. I'm here to talk to you about how to avoid the pitfalls again."

If no one raises their hand, it can be awkward, but you can easily follow up with, "No one? Perfect. I'm here to tell you how to avoid the many pitfalls involved if it should ever happen to you."

You might want to ask a rhetorical question instead. These questions don't require answers; they just get people thinking and serve as a stepping-off point for your presentation. For example:

*"Have you ever woken up in the middle of the night after a nightmare about a leveraged buyout? Chances are most of you have. I'll be glad to spend the next 45 minutes with you discussing ways either to avoid it completely, or to navigate its treacherous waters if it does happen."*

Rhetorical questions are wonderful for opening presentations. A bit later on in the talk, people may be more comfortable answering specific questions with a show of hands or even a verbal answer. If you choose this approach, consider leading up to the question with a statement like "At this point I think it would be interesting to see how many people agree that leveraged buyouts are getting more vicious as we speak."

All of these tools — stories, quotes, aphorisms, analogies, statistics, and questions — can be effectively employed throughout your presentation. Beware of using too many, in case your message becomes too complicated by the many ways you are putting it across, but also absolutely beware of not using them at all. They will help you begin your presentation in an interesting way, and will clarify the distinctions between your points. They will also help you end in a way that sends your message home in a memorable way.

 **Danger Zone**

Watch out for using these tools in your presentation but getting set in your ways. Remember to investigate your audience so that you make sure you are using analogies that will work for them, and questions that are pitched to their level.

## How else do we remember?

**Fast Fact**

Some things will be easier for your audience to remember than others.

You can make sure your listeners remember what you intend for them to remember in more ways than just the ones we have just looked at. We'll be looking at physical choices in Chapter 6, and in Chapter 7 we'll talk about your slides. But here's an interesting exercise before we move on. Try it out in a group:

**Try This**

Write down a list of 20 words. Make sure one of the words is repeated three times within the list. Have some unusual words in the list, and some compelling words. Ask a group of friends or family members to listen in a relaxed manner as you read your list out clearly and slowly. Tell them this is not a test to see how much they remember, but rather an exercise to see what people do remember. Once you've read out your list, have them write down the words they remember.

This exercise will show you how often people remember the first word on the list. This is called the primacy effect. They also often remember the last word, and this is called the recency effect. Naturally, they will recall the word that was repeated, and can often tell you how many times you said it as well! Beyond these words, some people will remember words they can relate to while others will remember words that they find unusual. It's hard to predict. So it's a good idea to include a mix of the familiar and the unusual in your text.

The fantastic thing about learning to employ the tools discussed in this chapter is that not only will your audience have an easier and more interesting time paying attention to and remembering your presentation, but also you will have more fun delivering it. When you introduce a strong verbal picture, you will see it yourself and it will guide you through your presentation. When you choose memorable words and place them effectively, they will continue to ring in your listeners' ears after you have finished speaking.

## Star Tips for using the words that will work best for you

1. Don't expect a group of adults to listen attentively for more than a 20-minute stretch. Use compelling language as a tool to get their attention back.

2. To be clear, interesting, and motivating, stick to words we all understand, and keep your sentences relatively short.

3. Be wary of using weak words, which can damage your credibility and lower your status.

4. Use the active voice to avoid sucking the life out of your message.

5. Remember that jargon is a completely foreign language to people outside the industry that developed them.

6. Rid your language of meaningless words and phrases such as "um", "you know", "actually", and "sort of". Doing so will make your presentations tighter and more compelling.

7. Add energy and interest to your presentation by using stories, aphorisms, analogies, statistics, and questions.

8. Use the power of primacy, recency, and repetition to make your word choices memorable.

# TOOLS FOR DELIVERY — YOUR VOICE

*"Words mean more than what is set down on paper. It takes the human voice to infuse them with shades of deeper meaning."*

Maya Angelou

4

## Your presentation toolbox

For odd jobs around the house, do you always use a hammer? Is it the only tool you have in your toolbox? If you need to tighten a screw or lift a floorboard, is that hammer effective?

Of course not. But this is the approach some people take to using their voice. No matter the situation, no matter the content, no matter the audience, they will use their voice in the same way, denying themselves the ability to construct a really powerful message and a meaningful relationship with their listeners.

Have you thought about your voice? Perhaps you've been told you have a pleasant one, or that you speak too softly sometimes. Maybe you've been asked to lower your voice when you feel passionate about something and start ranting. All of this information is very important for you as you develop your presentation style. Sometimes it's very important to speak softly, even in a presentation. Sometimes a rant is very effective. But if you are overwhelmingly inclined in either direction so that you always speak in a similar way, you're missing out on a huge opportunity for impact.

## Imitate your way to success

As babies, all of us learned to speak by imitation. It works really well! If you need to work on your ability to use your voice to great effect, start imitating again. Watch people delivering speeches on television, listen to interviews on the radio, trawl the Internet for audio or video recordings of speakers you admire. Start noticing where they choose to raise their volume, and what they do to emphasise words. Do they raise their pitch, or lower it? Do they slow down for emphasis? When do they speed up?

Once you have tuned your ear to listen for these techniques — some of which may be very natural to the speaker, some of which they may consciously be employing — try matching your voice to theirs. This is easiest to do with content on the Internet, as you can play a sentence, pause the video, and repeatedly imitate the way it was said. You can listen again, and try again, as many times as you need to.

While doing this, you need to look out for how it feels to you. If you are listening to a speaker you admire, but you find yourself feeling self-conscious and silly when you try to speak as emphatically as they do, you are discovering the size of your comfort zone.

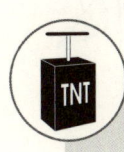

### Myth Buster

To improve as a speaker, I need to find a way to feel comfortable in front of an audience.

Not necessarily. It often works much better to focus less on your own comfort than on the comfort of your audience. If you pay attention to making your listeners comfortable, for example by controlling your voice in a way that makes you interesting and pleasant to listen to, your own comfort may well follow. Make your initial motivation the satisfaction of your listeners, not your own, and you will feel less self-conscious.

## Expanding your comfort zone

I think of my comfort zone as a hula-hoop that I'm standing inside. Every time I try something new that intimidates me, the hula-hoop gets bigger and the number of things I can do inside it increases. This doesn't mean that I'm totally comfortable doing everything inside the hoop, but I'm comfortable *enough* to give them another go.

It's best to practise in a safe environment before you take the leap in public, so here are a few vocal exercises to get you pushing at your hula-hoop. Knowing how one simple sentence can be made to mean many things when you use your voice to add weight to specific words will lead you to look at all your content in a new light.

### Try This

Say this sentence in a neutral way, without emphasis:

"I've got something very important to tell you."

Now, say it with emphasis on the word "I've". You can do this by raising the volume of your voice, or the pitch, or both. Can you hear how the sentence has a new meaning? You're telling your listeners that you and only you have this important message.

Now stress the word "something" as you say the sentence again out loud. The meaning changes a bit, doesn't it? Now your audience will feel intrigued by what this special something is.

Try it again. Emphasise "very". You're underlining the extent to which your message is important. You can also do this by emphasising "important".

Finally, repeat the sentence with emphasis on "you". The meaning changes completely. You're now highlighting how special your listeners are, and perhaps that you have chosen them to be the exclusive receivers of your message.

## But my material is so dry!

People complain about dry material a lot. Too much, in my opinion. If you choose robust language, employ tools like anecdotes and images, and add emphasis to your content with your voice, no material will be dry. Is it truly the material that is dry, or is it you?

Take a look at this paragraph:

> "In recent years, it has become apparent that fibre optics are steadily replacing copper wire as an appropriate means of telecommunications transmission. They span the long distances between local phone systems, as well as providing the backbone for many network systems. Other systems users include cable television services, university campuses, office buildings, industrial plants, and electric utility companies."

Dry? At first glance, yes. But read it through again with an ear for the words that would benefit from some emphasis on their meaning or importance. Now read it out loud, giving those words their due with your voice.

There are of course many ways to express these words, but if I were to do it, this would be my approach:

- I'd start by emphasising "recent". This is because I want to make sure that my listeners are clear on the time frame I'm talking about.

- I'd follow by emphasising "steadily". This will let them know that the trend is a strong one, and likely to continue.

- I'd draw out the word "long", to underline how much better fibre optic cable is than copper wire in this regard.

- It's important to hit phrases like "as well as", even though they can seem pretty neutral. They aren't at all. This one indicates that there are many advantages to fibre optics, and reminds your listeners to keep listening if they want to be clear on all of them.

- After that I'd add energy to the word "backbone". "Backbone" is the only analogy in the paragraph, and it calls up a great physical image.

- I'd raise the pitch of my voice on "Other" because the sentence is a list, and lists require a lot of energy. Watch out for lists as they can kill your presentation if you don't give each item its own vocal colour.

- Finally, my pitch would change a bit for each of the items on the list in the last sentence, to show my audience how important I feel each of them is.

 **Try This**

Try reading the paragraph out just like I've discussed. See how it feels.

Now do it again. Yes, presenting well takes practice! Stress each of the words so much that you feel uncomfortable. When you feel uncomfortable, it's probably just about right! Again, remember what we're going for here is audience satisfaction rather than your own ease.

To test the result, ask a friend or family member to listen to you deliver the paragraph with a lot of emphasis. Have them tell you how it sounds. Chances are they'll say it sounds great. If they say you've gone too far, tone it down a little and try again, knowing that you've succeeded in making your comfort zone hula-hoop bigger and are well on your way to refining your vocal tools. Pat yourself on the back.

**Aha! Moment**

There are so many ways to emphasise the words in any sentence. Making thoughtful choices for emphasis will add life and meaning to what I'm saying.

## Speed

People speak slowly, or quickly, for a wide variety of reasons. If you're like me, you tend to speed up your speaking pace when you are excited or tense. Other people will continue to speak slowly and quietly even when under pressure, perhaps in order not to frighten themselves.

If you start off your presentations speaking quickly, you have robbed yourself of the ability to use an increase in speed when you need to add energy or emphasis. Similarly, if you stick to a slow and consistent pace, you risk lulling your audience to sleep. Worse, you risk having them decide that you lack passion for your subject, as well as for the possibility of a fully engaged relationship with them.

### Fast Fact

People who speak slowly but smoothly, paying attention to the emphasis of their words, make the most impact.

Being a naturally fast speaker with an inclination to speed up when I'm excited, I've trained myself to slow down by focusing on how I enunciate my words. Particularly at the beginning of a presentation, it is important to give your listeners time to get used to your voice, to your accent, to your turn of phrase. Their minds are no doubt all over the place as you're starting. They're looking at your clothes, they're thinking about the meeting they've just come from, they are asking themselves if they're comfortable in the chair they chose or if the air is too cold or too warm. If you start off slowly, enunciating clearly, and giving yourself time to give your words the appropriate emphasis, you will be more successful at gathering their brains together.

In addition, slowing down your speech has the wonderful benefit of giving your brain the message that you have yourself under control. You're not sending panic messages to yourself, so your brain isn't sending more adrenalin to get you ready to fight or to flee. Everybody benefits.

### Try This

Here's the beginning of a presentation. Read it through silently, then read it out loud at your normal presenting speed.

"The other day I had a revelation. I suddenly realised that all the outlets in my house were bleeding energy

> that I wasn't benefiting from. This meant that I was bleeding money away for nothing. I'm here today to highlight to you how many bleeding outlets we have in our department, and what a straightforward and satisfying process it is going to be to channel that energy in useful ways."

Perhaps you placed more emphasis on some words than you normally might have because you've already been through the exercise we did a few pages ago. Great! But now I want you to slow your pace way, way down. I mean WAY down. Read it again. Listen to what happens.

Chances are that you discovered that by slowing down, you began to feel a stronger sense of the meaning of the sentences. And if you do, so will your listeners.

Speeding up is another story. For slower speakers, I wouldn't say it's absolutely necessary, because sometimes your mind simply processes things differently and speeding up might throw you off. What you do need to learn to do is to raise and lower your volume and play with your pitch, so that you sound motivated by and interested in your subject.

There was a very soft- and slow-spoken man named John in one of my workshops. He delivered a short presentation on how he felt it was important for the company to broaden its network of distributors, after which his colleagues gave him very clear feedback on his delivery. "Your voice, man," said one listener. "You're putting me to sleep!" After we talked about it for a while, I had John get up and deliver the first few lines of his presentation again, insisting that he stressed the importance of his message.

The difference was astonishing. After only the first sentence, his colleagues were nodding, and when he finished, we all clapped. "That was hard," he said. "It's not the way I talk at all." You may feel the same when you push yourself to be more expressive. But it's really worth it. He felt strange, but we, his listeners, were impressed, and months later, I still remembered what he said.

 **Aha! Moment**

In the end, my goal is to have my desired effect on the listener. It is much better to know that my words carry the power of my conviction than merely to hope they will speak for themselves without my help.

## Star Tips for making the most of your voice

1. Work on your ability to use your voice to great effect by imitating, just as you did as a baby.

2. It's best to practice in a safe environment before you try new things in public.

3. There's no such thing as dry material — only dry delivery.

4. Speak slowly and pay attention to the emphasis of your words to make the most impact.

5. Learn to raise and lower your volume and play with your vocal pitch; it will help you sound motivated by and interested in your subject.

# TOOLS FOR DELIVERY — YOUR FACE

5

"A good face is a letter of recommendation."

Proverb

## Face facts

Think about it. Where do we look when we want to judge whether or not someone is trustworthy, or credible, or intelligent, or kind? At their hands? At their knees? Of course not. We look at their face. And we pay particular attention to their eyes.

### Fast Fact

People who do not show expression on their face when they speak are much less convincing than those who do.

Have you ever heard a person's smile described as "not making it all the way to their eyes"? This means that the smile is false, doesn't it? So when we look for sincerity, the eyes are where we look. If you are saying you are happy to see me, but your eyes tell another story, I won't believe you. Similarly, if you are giving a presentation, trying to sell me on the benefits of a product or service, and I don't see conviction in your eyes, I may hesitate about committing to buy from you.

### Myth Buster

When we present, we experience lots of feelings, so our faces will naturally be expressive as a result.

Unfortunately not. Often our nerves cause us to limit our facial expressions, either because we are concentrating extremely hard or because we feel being expressive is a risk, and hope the words alone will deliver our meaning.

Many people become expressionless when they present because of nerves. They seem to feel it is a safer approach to take. The truth is the opposite. Not using your face to underline your message is a very dangerous choice to make. You are making it more likely that your message will be rejected rather than protecting yourself from rejection.

## Smile, and the world smiles with you

If you tend to be an emotionless presenter, learning to smile in appropriate places is a great place to start. You may in fact feel a certain intellectual happiness when you're telling a group of people that you are pleased to have the opportunity to talk to them, but unless you can express the emotional happiness to them, they won't feel it. Smile.

Somewhere in your presentation you may be delivering good news. Smile there as well! Some people are under the impression that presentations — no matter the content — are always a serious affair. I once trained a client who didn't smile in a part of his presentation that screamed for a smile. Without it, I didn't believe him at all. "But I'm not a smiley kind of guy," he said. "I don't care," I told him, "You have to think in terms of what will convince your audience, not what will make you feel safe."

Seriously folks, if you're not going to deliver your presentation as if you mean it, send it along as an e-mail instead. It might help you to remember that while your listeners are certainly listening to your presentation in order to decide how they feel about your opinion, your product, your service, or your company in general, they are also deciding how they feel about you. If they are potential clients, they will be wondering not only if they want to work with your company, but also if they want to work with you as an individual. If your face isn't credible, approachable, knowledgeable, and friendly, you could lose their business. It's likely that they will be listening to other proposals from other companies, and if the competition's presenter both sounds and looks more credible, you're at a big disadvantage.

You can also smile between sections of your presentation, as you pause to move from one subject to the next. Smile to show the group that you are still happy to be there with them. Perhaps take the opportunity to ask for questions. People will feel more inclined to engage with a smiling face than with a severe one, or even a neutral one. And engagement is what you're going for. Once you're engaged with your audience, everyone begins to feel better.

Your conclusion may be very serious. If so, I would never recommend that you deliver it with a smile. I would, however, recommend that after you deliver it, you make yourself available for discussion with a smile, so that people aren't afraid to talk to you.

 **Aha! Moment**

Sometimes my personality will be the deciding factor for a client. Developing my ability to be engaging with my facial expressions will give me an advantage over my competition.

## Closing and opening your face

Beyond smiling to express comfort and delight, there are many facial expressions that can add impact to your presentation. All the major emotions are fair game, and most of them involve a simple 'opening' and 'closing' of the face.

Take this paragraph, which was designed for use in a sales training programme:

> *"Let's take a moment to imagine what our competitors think about us. They think we're easy to displace because*

> *of our prices. They're saying to themselves, 'This will be a piece of cake. I'll just bid a bit lower and snatch away the business.' Imagine their surprise when our customers don't budge. Imagine their fury. Now they're thinking, 'What are sales all about if not about price?' I'll tell you what they're about. They're about being the best business partner in the industry."*

Of course this paragraph can be delivered in a neutral manner, just wearing a pleasant face. But imagine how much more interesting and memorable it will be with some emotion, particularly in the quotes. Look at it again.

> *"[Eyebrows raised — open face] Let's take a moment to imagine what our competitors think about us. [Eyebrows natural — credible face] They think we're easy to displace because of our prices. They're saying to themselves, [Eyebrows raised — gleeful face] 'This will be a piece of cake. I'll just bid a bit lower and snatch away the business.' [Eyebrows natural — amused face] Imagine their surprise when our customers don't budge. Imagine their fury. Now they're thinking, [Eyebrows down — angry, closed face] 'What are sales all about if not about price?" [Eyebrows natural — credible face] I'll tell you what they're about. They're about being more than a vendor. They're about being the best business partner in the industry."*

Where did all the emoting happen? Around the eyes. If you're like most humans (and no doubt you are) your eyebrows will have twitched while you read through the paragraph again, responding to the suggestions for expression. So since you've had this little rehearsal, now try reading it out loud, making the faces suggested.

How did that go? Feel okay? Again, you're unlikely to know how it went until you get some feedback.

### Danger Zone

Practicing in front of a mirror can actually be discouraging. It's unnatural to speak while looking in to one's own eyes, and we end up feeling more self-conscious than we do when speaking to another individual.

I always feel it's a good idea, when you try being more facially expressive, to find a colleague or friend who can let you know how you look. I also highly recommend setting up a camera and recording yourself as you try these things. The camera doesn't lie. Given that you are working on facial expressions, use quite a close-up shot. There's no need to see more than your head and shoulders. Learn a paragraph of text, like the example above, then deliver it the way you normally might. After that, use as many expressions as you can. Do it one more time, completely over the top. Then rewind, and watch all three.

When looking at your first reading, use your hand to cover the lower half of your face on the screen, so you can watch how your eyes behave. You may be surprised by how little they move.

My guess is that the second reading will look better to you than it felt. If it looks awkward, remember that it was a first effort, and you just need a little practice. I hope you will find the third, over-the-top reading amusing. But I'd also bet that while it might feel overdone, there will probably be parts of it that don't actually look overdone. What's more, you may well find that being more expressive with your face naturally leads to more vocal emphasis in those places as well. It's actually very hard to do one without the other.

Record yourself again, and again, and watch again. It's the only way to get to know yourself. We do so many things when we are speaking that we are unaware of, things that we don't see in the mirror when we are brushing our hair or shaving. Only a camera can introduce you to you. And only once you recognise how you truly look when you speak can you make helpful adjustments. Be prepared for some surprises. Not only do most of us find hearing our recorded voices extremely strange (*"I don't sound like that!"*) because we hear ourselves partially from the insides of our heads when we talk, we also notice mannerisms we had no idea we possessed when we see ourselves speaking on a screen.

I remember one participant in a training session taking his first look at himself, watching the replay of his presentation on his laptop. After just a few moments he closed his laptop cover and put his head down on his desk. "I am so boring," he groaned. He'd had no idea. But in fact this realisation was the best thing that could have happened. Faced with the reality of how monotonously and physically inexpressively he spoke while presenting, he became extremely committed to making positive changes.

It's also important to allow yourself to be charmed! In amongst the things you may not be happy with, there will be lots of things that work well. Your job is to be open to all of it, so that you can improve on your weaknesses and make good use of your strengths.

 **Aha! Moment**

Watching myself on camera will show me some very positive things about myself, as well as areas for improvement. It's all good!

## High brow, low brow

It's clear that a good number of our facial expressions involve raising or lowering our eyebrows:

**Shock**          **Pensiveness**          **Mock innocence**

**Sneakiness**          **Disbelief**          **Jealousy**

I'm sure that you can think of more. And now that you're thinking about it, you can start to work some of these expressions into your presentations to give them more life. An easy way to do so is to do as I did in the sample paragraph: add things people might think or say to your presentation so that you have to imitate their feelings. Allow yourself to have fun with it, and your audience will be entertained as well.

## The eyes have it

Some of our expressions don't involve such dramatic eyebrow gymnastics, of course. For example, if we want to express that we are feeling suspicious of something, we might narrow our eyes a bit. If we want to express that we are about to tell a secret, we might look left then look right, to show that we want to be sure no one unwanted is listening. For dismay or exasperation, we often roll our eyes to the ceiling.

Try some of these expressions in front of a camera as well. My favourite way to practice these things is to use a nursery rhyme like this one:

Mary had a little lamb
Its fleece was white as snow
And everywhere that Mary went
The lamb was sure to go.

### Try This

Try reciting this rhyme in front of a camera as if you are exasperated with the situation.

Now do it again as if you think it is the most wonderful thing that has happened to Mary, and you are delighted for her. Recite it a third time as if it's a big secret.

If you enjoy this challenge, take it a step further, as I do in my workshops. Have a friend listen to you reciting the rhyme with a strong emotion, then ask them if they could tell what emotion you were trying to express. Try showing that you're jealous of Mary, or find lambs disgusting, or that Mary and her silly lamb are boring you to tears. If your friend gets it right away, bravo! If not, don't tell them what you were trying to do, just keep trying until they get it. Expand your comfort zone hula-hoop as far as it needs to go to get your point across.

## Eye contact

You won't be as effective in your presentation, even if you are being expressive with your face, if you don't make eye contact with your listeners. Human instinct tells us not to trust someone who won't look us in the eye, so presenters who look over their listeners' heads or constantly at their laptop or screen will lose lots of points. While there may well be situations, depending on the culture or your relationship with the listeners, in which a lot of direct eye contact can work against you, the majority of listeners in the world today, be they CEOs, employees, or peers, want to be able to read your thoughts and feelings through your eyes.

Sometimes when we present, we are thinking so hard that we aren't really aware of where we are looking. We are 'seeing' our thoughts, so we're not very sensitive to where our eyes are going. We must learn to be aware of this. If not, we run the risk of offending, alienating, boring, or disappointing our listeners. There are several eye contact mistakes to watch out for.

### "Top Dog" syndrome

Presenters often know who the most powerful person in the room is, particularly at a meeting. This might be with a potential client, or at an important in-house gathering. Sometimes the presenter will look at that person and only at that person. Two things then occur: first, that person becomes very uncomfortable for being singled out and stared at for so long; second, the rest of the people in the room feel alienated or lose interest, or both. It's very important to be inclusive when you speak to a group. Practice looking at different people in the room, and being aware of doing it, during low-pressure situations, so that you can be sure to do it during higher-pressure ones.

### "It's Just You and Me" syndrome

In this case, presenters also look at only one person in the room, but it could be anybody at all. They do this not because they know that person has the power, but because they are too nervous to look anywhere else. If they look at someone they feel relatively comfortable with, then they reduce their nervousness a bit. The effect of doing so is the same as in Top Dog syndrome: intense discomfort for that person, and alienation for everyone else. It's also a clear indication of a lack of confidence, so presenters who do this appear very weak, which is distracting and uncomfortable for the listeners as well.

I find that the most helpful way in dealing with both of these tendencies is to greet people as they arrive, before the presentation. The more time you spend chatting with participants before you present, the more comfortable you will feel about looking them in the eye. If you've spoken to them before you start, you are also more likely to get a friendly look in return when your eyes meet. Everyone will be much more comfortable, and you will be judged more positively as a result.

**Danger Zone**

Not sharing your eyes with as many people in the room as possible will almost always be judged negatively — as nervousness, arrogance, or disrespect — by your audience.

## Big spaces: look, and your voice will follow

While it is difficult to make eye contact with listeners at the back of a large auditorium, they still need to feel you are looking at them, and doing so has an important added benefit. If you are looking at the back of a room, your voice will also travel there. First, you'll lift your head a bit to look at the people at the back, which will help your voice project. Second, staying aware of the people at the back will remind you to keep your volume at a level they can hear. If you only look at the people close to you, you will naturally adjust your volume for them, neglecting the rest of the room.

## Mouthing your way to success

You may also have noticed, watching the video of yourself being more expressive, that your mouth behaved differently. For example, when you decide to use your eyes to express suspicion, lowering your eyebrows and narrowing them, don't you find that your lips tighten a bit? When you raise your eyebrows and open your eyes to show surprise, doesn't your mouth open as well? Try expressing shock without your mouth following along. Very difficult!

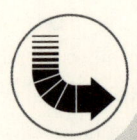 **Fast Fact**

When speaking to a large group, you will have more impact if you make your facial expressions more dramatic, opening your mouth more, or pursing your lips more fiercely, so that the expression travels the whole length of the room.

If you do a subtly sad face to make a point in front of a small group, you'll be understood, but if you do so in front of a group of 50 or 100, many in the room won't notice the change. It will have to be bigger. Go ahead and give them the full-lipped pout. You'll want to be able to support these emotions with your body as well...but that's coming up in the next chapter.

### Star Tips for adding meaning and impact with your face

1.  Make eye contact — it conveys sincerity.

2.  Employ facial expressions to underline your message.

3.  Recognise how you truly look when you speak so that you can make helpful adjustments.

4.  Smile, and the world smiles with you.

5.  'Open' or 'close' your face to convey all the major emotions included in your presentation.

6.  You can improve on your weaknesses and make good use of your strengths if you are open to everything you feel when you watch yourself on camera.

7.  Have fun with your facial expressions, and your audience will have fun too.

8.  Be conscious of where you are looking during your presentation.

9.  Make your facial expressions more dramatic when speaking to a large group, in order to reach everyone.

# TOOLS FOR DELIVERY — YOUR BODY

*"Emotion always has its roots in the unconscious and manifests itself in the body."*

Irene Claremont de Castillejo

## Do you speak body language?

No doubt you understand it. You can pick up on people's moods by the set of their shoulders, the restlessness of their hands, or the position of their feet. But how well do you speak it yourself? How clearly does your body speak when you present?

As discussed in the first chapter, if you are experiencing an overwhelming nervousness, that is the message that your body will be sending to your listeners, and it may be speaking more loudly than your voice. It is very important that you work on your nervousness in order to regain control of your body, and then that you take a good look at your body language in order to use this wonderful physical tool to underline your message and maintain audience attention.

You won't be surprised that I'm going to tell you to video yourself again. This time zoom out so that your whole body is in the frame. Now deliver a section of your presentation to the camera. It makes sense to record your introduction and perhaps the first section of your presentation, to get a good idea of how you behave at the beginning and during a transition to the first section of your talk.

I highly recommend that you do this right now, if possible. Don't continue reading until you've recorded yourself, so that you can assess yourself as you are right at this moment.

## Putting the body puzzle together

### Feet

You'll be tempted to watch your face first, but let's start with your feet and work our way up. Are they planted firmly, with both heels on the floor? If so, fantastic. This is a great way to start, literally grounded in your opening. Watch out that your toes are not turned inward — something most commonly done by women — as this conveys childishness and lack of certainty. Toes turned rather far outward also looks less strong, and can be distracting.

A lot of people cross one leg over the other when they are uncertain in front of a group. As usual, this is a very basic self-protective instinct. Unfortunately, it gives our nerves away, and it also destabilises us. We're very easy to push over in this position, and we look it. If this is your tendency, fight it. Remember how much it can help to plant your feet and clench your thigh and buttock muscles to give you a sense of confidence and deal with the shakes.

If you are a woman wearing heels, watch out for the tendency many of us have to turn one foot out to the side and lift the toes. It can be okay to do so later on in your presentation, once you have established yourself, but I'd say it has no place at the beginning.

## Knees

If your feet are moving around a lot at the beginning of your presentation, they are in cahoots with your knees. Adrenalin will make them want to wiggle. Clenching your thigh muscles will address this issue as well.

## Hips

Look at the centre of your body. Is it straight up and down, or are you cocking a hip to one side or the other? Are you standing with your pelvis thrown forward? Make an effort to keep your hips level, in line with your feet. You will feel stronger, and the audience will also see you that way.

## Back and shoulders

How's your posture? Our lack of certainty in the beginning can sometimes cause us to slouch, dropping our shoulders forward in a deferential, self-protective gesture. Even letting your shoulders drop a few centimetres can make a huge difference in the message you are sending about yourself, your subject, and your organisation.

Maybe you don't slouch only when you present. Maybe you're a chronic sloucher. This is true of many of us as we age, and it's certainly something to work on. Not only will better posture lead to changes in how people receive your message, but it will also help you avoid back, shoulder, and neck strain. The more you take care of your health, the more likely people will be to want to work with you.

 **Danger Zone**

Our posture has a tendency to deteriorate as we age. Keep an eye on yours so that it doesn't.

## Arms and hands

One of the reasons I asked you to look at your feet first is that we worry so much about where to put our hands that we forget entirely about how our feet are feeling and what they do. But now let's look at your arms and hands. What have they decided to do while you're talking?

If they are calm, and move about in order to add appropriate emphasis to your message, consider yourself a natural. However, many of us have to work on looking comfortable in front of a crowd, and we need our arms and hands to be relaxed in order to do so.

I consistently get this question: "Where should I put my hands? I feel like such a lump just letting them hang there by my sides! But anything else feels awkward. What works?"

The answer is that different things work for different people, so you will have to figure out what works for you. Here are a few examples of what you can do, and what you should be aware of if you decide to adopt them.

## Hand in pocket

Some people look fine with a hand in a pocket at the beginning, gesturing with the other hand until they are comfortable enough to use both. If you choose this position, though, remember to take the hand back out of the pocket after a while. It's odd to use only one hand for too long. Also, take anything you might be inclined to fiddle with out of your pockets.

## Crossed arms

Some people believe you must never cross your arms during a presentation, as it looks too defensive or aggressive, but I avoid saying never when it comes to bodies. Some people look aggressive when they cross their arms because they are aggressive. Some people, particularly women, cross their arms with their hands high up on their upper arms, as if they are protecting their breasts. Other people look relaxed and thoughtful when they do so. If you are starting your presentation off with some rhetorical questions, maybe crossing your arms will work. Try it in front of the camera and see how it looks. After a while, gesticulate with one of your hands and arms. Then, when you want to be even more expressive, let both arms loose.

## Hands behind your back

There are people who look great and feel good with their hands behind their back. Others look too military, or too childlike. Check it out for yourself. I find that putting my hands behind my back is a nice position for me during a question and answer session, as it shows that I am listening, taking a back seat while my listeners talk. But there are certainly other times in a presentation where you can make it work for you as well.

## Hands on hips

What about putting your hands on your hips? Too aggressive? Absolutely not. It all depends on how you do it. When you put your hands on your hips you make yourself look bigger; this will have the effect of expressing strength. But of course you can also do it if you are role-playing in your presentation. Maybe you're imitating an irate client or a stubborn negotiator. Play around with it!

### One arm hanging, one arm holding the other

Maybe it's your choice to leave one arm hanging down at your side and to hold onto it with the opposite hand? This pose is an instinctive effort to protect the stomach from possible attack, and as a result it broadcasts weakness and uncertainty. I recommend avoiding it.

### Both hands in front of the groin

Another pose that indicates a feeling of vulnerability is the one where the presenter holds both hands in front of the groin, like a soccer player lined up to defend against a free kick. It can seem like a neutral, comfortable pose to the presenter, but watch out for coming across as defensive as a result.

### The opera singer

Do you bend your arms and hold your hands in front of your belly like an opera singer? A lot of people do this when presenting, and it works well for plenty of them, but it can also look a bit unnatural. Most of this has to do with how long you do it for, and what  your hands are doing at the time. If your hands are holding each other so tightly that your knuckles are turning white, it's probably best to find another position. If you are playing with your rings, you're broadcasting nervous energy. Deal with your adrenalin, and calm your appendages.

 **Myth Buster**

There are some positions we must never use when we are presenting.

This is true to a certain extent, but the number of these positions is probably smaller than you think. Everything depends on how, and when, you use them.

## How many words are there in your body language vocabulary?

Even if your feet are nicely planted, your legs and arms are calm, and your posture is good, you might be undermining your impact by using the same gesture over and over. One client of mine chose to place the tips of his fingers together so that his hands made a tent shape, and reached out like this toward his listeners to emphasise his points. This wouldn't be a problem from time to time, but that gesture has no obvious meaning, and repeated incessantly it becomes ridiculous. We worked together on expanding his body language vocabulary.

## Try This

I'm going to write a list of words here that have hand gestures that most people will understand, even internationally. I want you to imagine the hand gesture as you read them. Go ahead and do the gesture. Is it one you ever use? Try and work it into your physical vocabulary, so your hands can be comfortable speaking this way.

Together

Separate

Balanced

Mixed

Love

Cut

Advance

Reduce

Grow

There are certainly several ways to use gestures to indicate these meanings. The goal is to find one that works for you and for your audience. And remember, when speaking to a bigger crowd, be sure to make the gesture bigger as well.

## Fast Fact

People from different cultures sometimes interpret body language in different ways. For example, the 'thumbs up' sign is considered to be a very foul gesture in some Middle Eastern countries. Research acceptable body language if you present internationally.

## The complete message

Putting all the pieces of your body together into a coherent message may seem like a big job, but half the battle is won by being very convinced of what your message is in the first place. Once you are clear in your mind and in your heart of the importance of what you have to say, then your voice, your face, and your body will know what to do to get that message across. If you're unsure of the message, your body will let everyone know.

This reminds me of a story a friend told me about her experience in a horse show as a nine-year-old child. She was leaving the dressing room to go out to the ring, and was nervously checking that her riding clothes were hanging right and her hair was in place. A woman who knew her and had noticed her anxiety approached her and said, "You'll do much better if you stop focusing on yourself and think about the pony."

This is true of presenting. Focus on your message, not on how you feel about yourself, and you will perform much, much better in the ring.

Just like training your body for a sport takes practice and regular attention, training yourself to present well does too. You would never train to compete in tennis by only practising your forehand. Don't expect to do well in presentations by working on only some of your tools for delivery and not others.

 **Danger Zone**

We think that if we have good slides or handouts and a voice, we're done.

Delivering a successful presentation is a full-body experience. It's a workout. If you're not exhausted at the end, it's likely you've left some of your most important tools behind.

## Star Tips for making effective physical choices

1. Use your body language to underline your message and maintain audience attention. Every part of your body has a message.

2. Find hand and arm positions that work best for you.

3. Avoid using the same gesture over and over as this can undermine your impact.

4. When speaking to a bigger crowd, make your gestures bigger as well.

5. Focus on your message, not on how you feel about yourself, and you will perform much better.

# VISUAL AIDS
# THAT HELP
# RATHER THAN HURT

*"Simplicity is the ultimate sophistication."*

Leonardo da Vinci

## What's the point?

Not everyone learns best when the information is presented verbally, so we use visual aids to make our message clearer and more memorable. As you probably know, in most modern business presentations, the primary audiovisual aid consists of slides developed on a laptop and projected onto a screen, using software such as PowerPoint or Keynote. Presenters also use flipcharts and whiteboards, and sometimes props such as toys or scale models as well.

All of these aids, when used well, can be a great help to a presentation. Unfortunately, they can also damage it.

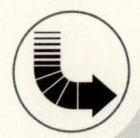 **Fast Fact**

You must be able to survive without your slides.

## The slippery nature of slides

Before we get into the do's and don'ts of how to develop your slides, I'd like you first to think about the role they play in your presentations. What I want to know is: Are your slides your presentation?

If the answer is yes, please beware. Beware for two reasons. The first is technical; the second is psychological.

### Technical problems

There are so many potential technical hiccups when your slides are your presentation: your laptop can fail, your projector can fail, the electricity can fail, you can bring the wrong version of your slides, your laptop can be stolen, you can forget the cord that connects your laptop to the projector. Ask any presenter with a lot of experience, and I'm sure they will have at least one story about something on this list.

I certainly do. I once discovered while setting up for a 90-minute talk that my password no longer unlocked my laptop. There was nothing to do but go on with the talk, describing the slides as vividly as possible, not allowing myself to worry about the situation. I realised that not having the slides, most of which were images, forced me to use a very descriptive vocabulary, and to express myself with extra energy. At the end of the session, one of the participants asked me to send her the slides by e-mail so she could see them anyway. I did so, and received this message from her in response: "After looking through your slides, it dawned on me how you described the images so perfectly — you didn't need the slides at all!"

Now, if your subject is intensely technical or full of numerical data, you can't necessarily be expected to remember all the details by heart. But if for some reason you arrive at a meeting or a conference and your slides don't work, you are very unlikely to get another chance to present. You've got to have the confidence that you can deliver your most important points and information without them. If you've been through the content development process we discussed in Chapter 2, and if you've rehearsed, you're likely to have the basics of your presentation planted very firmly in your mind and will be able to deliver a sufficiently informative presentation.

My recommendation to all presenters is to practise their presentation at least once as though their laptop has failed and the show must nonetheless go on. When you do so, not only might you discover that you remember much more of it than you imagined you would, but you will also develop other very useful techniques for getting your information across. Maybe you'll decide that it makes sense to use a flipchart for some of your talk, even if your slides do work, because you've practiced using a flipchart instead and it provides a nice change and an opportunity to develop an idea step by step. All sorts of things can happen when you force yourself to be creative and trust your brain to deliver.

## The psychological issue

Seeing how much it helps to practice your presentation without your slides will show you how depending wholly on your slides means you have less faith in your ability to manage the information and the delivery without them as a crutch.

 **Danger Zone**

> You can easily become a slave to your slides, rather than their master.

Being the master of one's presentation slides requires a change in mindset for a lot of people, but the effort pays off in spades. The benefits are very powerful:

- You become aware of how much simpler your slides could be. Therefore...

- You have more confidence in your ability to manage the information.

- You look at your slides when you need to be prompted, rather than read them. Therefore...

- You are willing to come out from behind your laptop to engage your listeners.

## Slides to open with, slides to close with

Watching most business presentations these days, I spend so much time looking at Agenda slides and Closing Comments slides, followed by the mind-numbing "Thank You" slide. I know that many, many companies have established corporate presentation templates, and I agree that it makes good sense to have the look and feel of corporate presentations be consistent. But it's also important to think hard about the effect of a very predictable slideshow.

## Opening slides

Yes, it helps to have an agenda, so that your listeners recognise whether they will be listening to what they came to listen to. However, it can be quite boring to automatically put up your agenda slide first, particularly when most presenters simply put it up and read out to their listeners from the screen.

Think about the message this sends. First, it shows that you haven't derived a strong overall theme for your presentation, merely a list of subjects to cover. Second, it indicates that you aren't the master of your presentation because you need to read the list. And finally, it shows your listeners that you are more comfortable looking at the screen than at them, right from the start.

Consider having your first slide be an image that represents your main objective. Tell them what you are there to do — what you are there to educate them on, to convince them of, to frighten them with, to galvanise them about — and then use your agenda to tell them exactly how you are going to do it. Also consider bringing only one agenda item up at a time, so that you can address it without your listeners reading ahead. You really need to grab their attention at the beginning in order to keep it, and memorising your agenda and delivering it in an interesting fashion is a great way to do this.

Supporting each agenda item with an image or an icon that you use again when you reach that part of the presentation can also be interesting, memorable, and effective.

**Fast Fact**

Your listeners can read faster than you can talk. Revealing agenda items one by one is the best technique; otherwise they will be reading ahead instead of listening to you discuss each one.

## Closing Comments

Because presenters know they need to close their presentation, and because it seems to make sense to do so with final comments, we are now seeing some really tedious Closing Comments slides out there.

Just like an agenda, they don't need to be tedious, but they so often are. Either they are a mere repetition of what has been said, or, bizarrely, they introduce something completely new without going into it. Done either way, it is a lost opportunity for impact.

### Myth Buster

Putting up a slide entitled 'Closing Comments' will get people's attention.

Most listeners know that if they've been paying attention all along, they can predict the closing comments. So instead of paying attention, they start to think of what is next on their schedule. And if they do decide to pay attention anyway, and your comments are a mere repetition of what you've said so far, their final memory of your presentation will be quite a dull one.

We discussed various options for closing in Chapter 2. It's not at all a mistake to repeat your main points, as long as you do so in a very tight fashion, but it is far more effective to do so in conjunction with a link to the question you used to open your presentation with, or an anecdote, or a final arresting image. This gives the presentation an extra bit of energy at the end, and leaves the listeners with a smile, or some good food for thought.

Here's a great example. Serene was developing a presentation about mobile telephone applications for a conference. Her final message to the audience had to do with the difficulty of developing what she referred to as a "killer application". In order to illustrate the idea, she thought of using a photo of a great white shark. Clever idea, right? She put the photo of the shark lunging open-mouthed at the camera on the bottom right part of the slide, and above it she wrote: "The most important thing to know about the killer application is ... there is no killer application."

At first glance, the slide looked great, and the message was clear and provocative. It was really something for the audience to think about. But the problem was that in designing the slide this way, Serene had designed her way out of a job. She spelled out her message, and the audience would have read it before she even finished saying the first half of it.

A simple, powerful message like that is easy enough to memorise, and listeners do not need to see the words to feel their impact. My recommendation to Serene was to remove the words from the slide entirely, and to enlarge the photo of the shark so that it filled the whole screen. This would allow her to bring up the slide of the shark, and let her listeners take in the image. Since this was the concluding slide of her presentation, she could then take the opportunity to approach her audience and grab their attention with her words. She said, "Everyone out there is looking to develop the killer application, one that will take the mobile technology world by storm. The most important thing to know about killer applications is this ... (pause) ... There is none."

Leaving the words on the slide would have meant that Serene was playing the role of the slide's servant, standing by its side to support its message. By changing her slide and her approach, Serene was able to become master of her message, to have the slide support *her* in a really strong conclusion. She spoke for herself.

 **Fast Fact**

You are your presentation! Your presentation is not your slides!

## Call to action

If your presentation has been an effort to convince your listeners of something, then the whole idea of closing comments is inappropriate. Your goal has been to change their mindset and motivate them in a new direction, so if you don't end with a call to action you won't be striking while the iron is hot.

Imagine, for example, that you've just made a presentation to a potential client about how, based on your research into their needs, your company is perfectly placed to offer solutions that will help drive their business. You've done a very good job of laying out both the current market conditions and their specific challenges, and you've shown how helpful your company can be in addressing these challenges. At the end, you bring up a Closing Comments slide. Is this going to motivate them to agree to work with you? It might not. Why take the risk?

Instead, if you finish the body of your presentation, and recap briefly and clearly why your company and theirs would make such perfect partners, you can capitalise on the momentum by saying something like, "As a result, what I'd really like to do now is to sit down with you and your logistics manager to see how quickly we can set a transition to our logistics system in motion. Can we make an appointment for this to happen?" Or you could say, "If you are as convinced as I am of the benefits of a partnership, it would be great to take some time now to discuss any issues you might have with the idea, so that I can come back to you with a very concrete proposal."

You don't want to walk away with a non-committal "Thanks for coming, we'll be in touch." Your boss will naturally ask you, "When?" If you develop an engaging call to action, you are unlikely to leave the meeting without some sort of commitment, whether it be for something as small, but important, as a research meeting with another relevant party, or as big as a contract.

**Aha! Moment**

Every meeting provides the opportunity to create forward momentum. When I simply restate my main points in my concluding remarks, I miss the opportunity to make things happen.

## Trends in presentation slides

When PowerPoint first burst onto the scene, it was all the rage to use all its animation tools to make colourful, lively slides. Words bounced in from the left, pictures spun in from the right, one slide dissolved into another.

These days, however, people have realised that all that activity actually detracted from the message rather than solidified it. Too much animation and too much colour are a liability. People may have emotional reactions to these details that will get in the way of your message. A little goes a very long way. Let's take a look at the general parameters for what does and doesn't work.

## Slide do's and don'ts

| Do's | Don'ts |
| --- | --- |
| Keep your colour scheme simple | Confuse the eye with too much variety |
| Favour black words on a white ground | Make your audience work to read your words |
| Stick to one message per slide | Pack your slides with words and data |

| Do's | Don'ts |
|------|--------|
| Limit the number of words per point | Write in lengthy, full sentences |
| Use clear and interesting images | Put too many competing images on one slide |
| Build your slides point by point | Bring up all your bullets at once |
| Use appropriate video or audio tools | Expect these options to make up for a weak presentation |

**Aha! Moment**

If I put too much on my slides, I'll diminish my own impact and steal my own thunder!

## The good, the bad, and the ugly

Slide 7.1.1 on the facing page is from a presentation on techniques for cleaning semiconductor wafers. See what you think.

At first glance, it seems quite clear. Look again, though. Notice the unnecessary numbers before each item. It looks as if it has been lifted out of a document without any adjustments. Even in a document, there aren't enough items to justify all these section numbers. You don't want your slides to remind your listeners of being in a boring school lecture!

When you read through the text, you'll see that it's needlessly repetitive. Because of this, there are many more words than there need to be, and this means that the image has to be quite small. What's more, there are inconsistencies in the use of fonts and capitalisation, so the overall look of the slide is a bit messy. When you open this slide, both you and your listeners are likely to feel a bit anxious. Simplifying this slide (slide 7.1.2) will make it much easier to understand and to present.

## CLEANING

- **2.3 Wafer Rinsing and Drying Techniques:**
  - **2.3.1 Type of wafer rinsing techniques:**
  - **2.3.1.1 Overflow Rinsers:**
    - Overflow techniques is used to mainly:
      - Remove cleaning chemical on the wafer surface.
      - Remove particles on wafer surface.
    - This rinsing is done in a overflow bath with continuous DI water supply from bottom of the tank. The bath is filled up until overflowing occurs.
    - DI water flow range : 25 to 35 l/min.

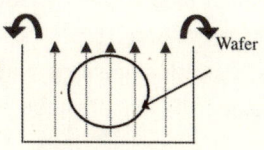

**Overflow bath diagram**

Slide 7.1.1

---

**CLEANING**: Wafer Rinsing and Drying Techniques

Overflow rinsers remove cleaning chemicals and particles on the wafer surface.

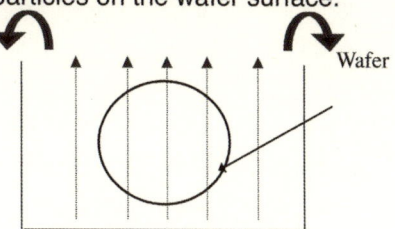

Wafer

Continuous DI water supply

## DI water flow range: 25 to 35 l/min.

Slide 7.1.2

Removing the repetition in the text has made it possible to keep the slide to the one main point, to increase the size of the image, and make the numerical information bigger and clearer. I'm sure you can see how this slide gives the presenter the opportunity to talk without constantly referring to the words, and provides information that is very easy for the listener to remember.

Now look at the next two slides on the facing page. The first (slide 7.2.1) is packed with information. With this much on the slide, what role does the presenter play? It's not clear. The listeners can read what's on the screen themselves. And it's obvious the presenter wants the slide to function as a take-home document as well. There is no way a listener can take in and remember all those numbers.

Again, I'd recommend paring the slide down to its central point or image (slide 7.2.2), adding memorable data, and taking the opportunity to talk about what the various projects in the effort are like. Tell your listeners that they will have all the figures in the handouts you have prepared for them.

Alternatively, if you feel that for the purposes of discussion you must have all the figures from all four of the projects up on the slide, bring them up one at a time, so that you build the story you are telling, and don't overwhelm your audience.

## Handouts

A lot of people like to receive handouts to remind themselves of the details of a presentation once it is done. Some clients will insist upon having handouts provided, but you might want to prepare some for clients who don't as well, particularly if your presentation is heavy with data, so you don't have to put all the information your listeners are interested in up on your slides. (There's more on this in the following chapter on technical presentations).

*Slide 7.2.1*

*Slide 7.2.2*

A problem with handouts is that if you give them out at the beginning of your presentation, the people who prefer to read rather than to listen will not pay attention to you. They will take your information in and draw their own conclusions from it, and you will be denied the opportunity to shape their perception to your own. You will also look out at the tops of many heads as they read, rather than into their eyes, so you won't be getting any signals from them about their comprehension or opinions.

It's best to let them know that they will be able to pick up handouts as they leave the room at the end of your presentation. They will then know that they won't necessarily have to take notes if they don't want to, and will keep their eyes on you.

## Conference and workshop handouts

Much of the world has been deforested in order to fill conference binders and provide training workshop handouts of limited value. How many times have you opened a conference binder to discover that these 'notes' are merely printouts of the presenters' slides? Conference organisers aren't helping, in fact, because they often simply ask for a copy of your slides rather than anything more richly informative for the listener. The same goes for a lot of trainers. They print up their slides, put them in a folder, and call it your workshop handbook.

Perhaps you will argue with me that printing up your slides gives your listeners ample opportunity for note-taking in their own way in the empty space around the slide. Indeed it does. And naturally there are instances where a copy of the presenter's slides is all that is needed. If what you want your listeners to have is purely factual, and your slides are clear in presenting the facts, then of course that's fine. What's missing in many instances, however, is the added value of making your conference or workshop handouts into truly valuable documents that will remind the participants not just of the big picture but also of the finer details of what you offered. What's more, unlike slides, handouts give you the opportunity to have your listeners get involved in the talk by filling in blanks that make them think, taking quizzes, or writing down their thoughts during group discussions.

**Try This**

Ask yourself, "If the participants look at my handouts a year from now, will they be reminded not only of my main points and examples but also of associated information as well as their own participation in the discussion?"

Let's look at an example of how three slides (slides 7.3.1 – 7.3.3) and their corresponding handout page (handout 7.4) can be very different, to good effect.

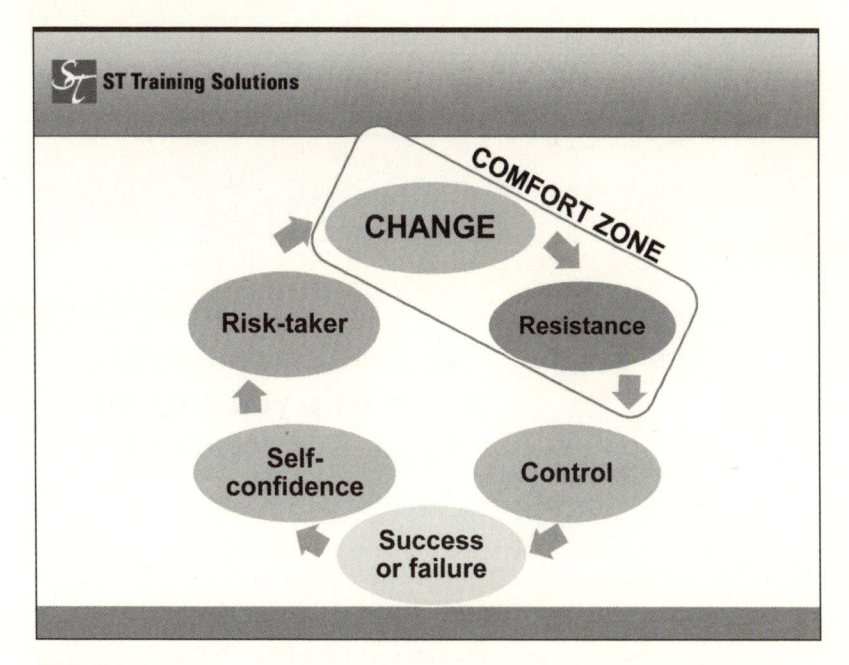

*Slide 7.3.1*

**ST Training Solutions**

**X** (terrified)

**COMFORT ZONE**

**X** (slightly anxious)

**Definition:**
A limited set of behaviours that a person will engage in without becoming a*nxious*.

Alternatively described as a p *lateau*, it describes a set of behaviours that have become comfortable, without creating a sense of r*isk*.

*Slide 7.3.2*

 **ST Training Solutions**

**What action could you take to help you step out of your Comfort Zone?**

 If you always do what you always did, you'll always get what you always got. If you want something different, CHANGE!

*Slide 7.3.3*

# The Change Cycle and You

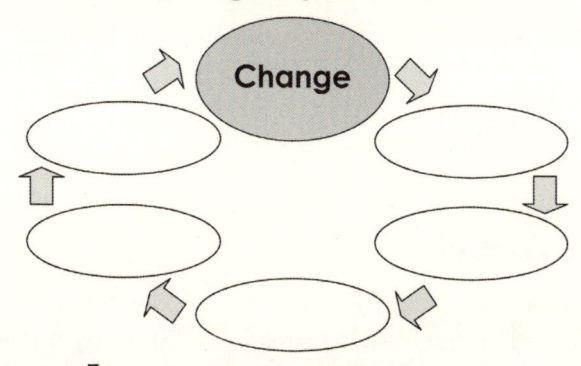

The **C**_____ **Z**_____ is a limited set of behaviours that a person will engage in without becoming **a**_____. Also described as a **p**_____, it describes a set of behaviours that have become comfortable, without creating a sense of **r**_____.

**Highly successful people routinely step outside their comfort zones to accomplish what they wish.**

Are you sticking so close to what you are good at that you are limiting your path forward? If you stay in your comfort zone too long, you will end up on your own!

**Your comfort zone will become very uncomfortable!**

### What action could you take to help you step out of your Comfort Zone?

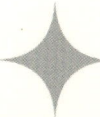

**If you always do what you always did, you'll always get what you always got. If you want something different, CHANGE!**

*Corresponding handout 7.4*

Notice how the slides are designed to let the presenter gradually develop the topic as details are elicited from the participants. The handout page allows participants to think as they listen and discuss. Writing in the important words will also help them to remember, and there's a space provided for jotting down notes from the group discussion. The handout also offers related information for further study.

## Remote control

If you generally stand during your presentations, I hope you've invested in a remote control so that you don't have to keep returning to your laptop to advance your slides. You don't necessarily need one if you are seated at a table with a small number of people, looking at your laptop screen rather than at a screen on the wall. Not having one when you stand to present, however, means that you are either constantly leaving and approaching your laptop, which limits your ability to give a smooth presentation both verbally and physically, or sticking by your laptop the whole time, which is even more limiting. What's more, I find that most people like to use their right hand to tap their laptop, but place their laptop somewhere to their listeners' left. This means that they have to turn their body away from their listeners to advance their slides.

Here are a few simple rules of thumb to follow when using a remote control:

- If your remote control isn't working or you forgot to bring it along, remember to put your laptop in a place you can access without turning your body away from your listeners.

- When holding the remote control but not actively using it, be aware of what your hands are doing. Quite often, presenters unconsciously fiddle with it, then get a shock when they see that they've been changing slides as they talked. Consider putting it down when you know you won't need it for a long stretch of talking.

- Keep extra batteries in your laptop bag so that you don't get caught with a useless remote.

## Laser pointers

I rarely see laser pointers used well. Most often, I feel that presenters use them because then they don't have to think about what to do with their hands. Also, because the pointers are often attached to the remote control for changing slides, presenters feel they might as well use them.

The problem is that so many people point to something on their slide by circling it with the laser pointer rather than simply pointing at it. It's called a laser pointer, not a laser *circler*. When you make the laser point go around and around or bob between things on the screen, it is harder on the listener, not easier. It doesn't bother you, because you know what you are referring to, but if you are asking your listeners to follow the pointer, do your best to keep it still so that they can focus on what's on the slide, not on the movements of the little red dot.

I feel that laser pointers are best employed in conference situations where you are dealing with a very large screen. But even then it might not be ideal because the laser point could be too small to see by the people in the back of the room. In such cases, it helps a lot to work highlighting into your slides. If you are in front of a small enough group and projecting your slides onto a normal-sized screen, I highly recommend that you approach the screen and indicate what you are talking about with your hand. Of course, when you do this, you must avoid turning your back to your audience. Use whichever hand allows you to gesture to the screen while keeping your face to your listeners.

 **Fast Fact**

Moving to the screen and interacting with the content of your slides in order to be clear to your listeners adds energy and interest to your presentation. People like to watch presenters move around, and stay interested longer as a result.

## Flipcharts and whiteboards

I'm so glad that laptop-based presentations haven't meant the end of flipcharts and whiteboards. They are very versatile tools. It's important to have one or the other on standby, in case something goes wrong with your laptop or projector, but even if your technology works well, using flipcharts and/or whiteboards as well can be very effective during your presentation.

### Flipchart fun

Flipcharts aren't for you if you have illegible handwriting or aren't patient enough to draw things carefully, but if you like writing your points on paper as you talk, by all means, use them.

There are a few things to watch out for:

- Use pens in bold colours that have wide enough tips so that what you write can be seen from the back of the room.

- Use dark colours to write and bright colours to highlight if you need to. People will have trouble reading if you write in light green or pink or yellow.

- Your body will naturally block the words you are writing as you write, so it is best to write, step to the side, and talk about what you've written. If you are right-handed and are standing on the flipchart's right, every time you point at something with your right hand you will have to turn your body away from your listeners. Try to point with your left hand so that you keep your body facing them.

Here are some ways of using flipcharts:

### Diagrams

If you are using a lot of diagrams, it makes very good sense to buy your own flipchart paper and prepare them ahead of time. If you have just a few you'd like to use to illustrate a point, it's a really nice visual diversion to draw them on the spot. You'll keep your listeners interested by giving them something different to look at and a different way to think. It gives you an opportunity to move to a different part of the room, and refreshes the energy a bit.

### Drawing on the spot

If you're not a great artist but really like the idea of doing a drawing on the spot, you can try a nice little trick some presenters use and draw the diagram lightly in pencil beforehand. Your audience won't be able to see the pencil lines, but you'll be close enough to follow them. You'll look like an artist, and they'll never know!

### Group work

Flipcharts are fantastic for encouraging participation in your presentations. If you'd like to get people thinking and sharing ideas, you can break into groups and give each group a flipchart for writing down their ideas. People who hesitate to offer their ideas in large groups are often more comfortable speaking up in a small one. After brainstorming, groups may stick their flipchart paper on the wall, so each group can give their feedback to all the participants and share their discussions, and everyone will benefit from the list of points each group has made. You can also take what they have written back to the office with you after your presentation, either to be incorporated into further presentations, or to include in a follow-up e-mail to those participants.

### Whiteboard pros and cons

One advantage of a whiteboard is that it is usually bigger than a flipchart, so you can build much more information on it. Also, you can write things that require correction and make the changes by erasing and rewriting. Lots of listeners find this helps them learn and remember. Whiteboards have another characteristic that flipcharts don't: you can stick things on them. If you like to put up posters to provide information and enliven the room during your presentation, but don't want to damage the walls, stick them up on the whiteboard.

The disadvantage of course is that once it is full, you have to erase everything to write more information down. Also, you can't take it away with you if there's something on it worth keeping.

## Fun and games

Beyond these traditional visual aids, there are many more being used to great effect by presenters and trainers all over the world. The sky's really the limit when it comes to illustrating your point and getting people to think along with you. No doubt you can come up with your own as you continue to develop your goals and your understanding of your audience. Here are some that work very well, to get you started.

### Blank cards

Shirley Taylor and I use these in lots of our workshops, to get a feeling from the whole group as to their current concerns following small group discussions. So, for example, in my presentation skills workshop, I will ask small groups of four or five people to develop a list of what they find are the main obstacles to presenting successfully. Once they've discussed this, I give each group three large index cards and a big magic marker and ask them to agree on the top three obstacles on their list. Then I collect all the cards and stick them up on the wall in related groups. In this way I can see what the main concerns of this particular group are, and we can keep referring to these issues as we go through the training.

### Pictures

An image trainer I know uses packs of cards with a huge assortment of photographs on them. During her training sessions she gives a pack to each small group and asks them to spread the cards out on the group's table, then each participant is asked to choose the pictures they feel represent their personality most. The visual stimulation from this exercise is wonderful, and it's really interesting to see what everyone chooses for themselves, so people are engaged and motivated to participate.

## Words

In one of her talks on communication skills, Shirley Taylor uses A4 cards printed with one word each to get people involved and learning. Before the talk, she sometimes sticks them randomly under chairs, and then during the talk she will ask everyone to reach under their chair to see if they have a card there. She asks people who have cards to come up to the front of the room, and to arrange themselves into a sentence using the words on their cards. Otherwise she just hands out the cards as she's talking. It's great fun for the rest of the audience to watch the process, and a very nice platform for learning.

## Toys

I once attended a presentation where there was a little toy waiting on each chair, and have been to several where there have been toys or balloons on the tables. In the first case, the goal of the presenter was to get our brains into a playful, positive mode while we waited for him to start. In the second instance, the toys were part of an exercise during the presentation that illustrated an important point, and of course woke us up as well. One of my professors in a college astronomy class attached his little son's toys to a long, sturdy elastic rope and got two students to pull the ends of the rope in order to illustrate

the way the universe is understood to expand. In all these instances, the toys served to heighten our interest before or during the presentation, and made many of us smile.

### Danger Zone

If you put toys out for use at the beginning of a presentation and don't use them later on, your listeners may prefer to fiddle with them than to listen to you. Ask for them back, or request your listeners to put them under their chairs once they have served their purpose.

## Visual aids for you

Even if you have a set of slides and the ability to look at your laptop screen for reminders, you may feel the need to use notes. It's great not to need to, and it's worth working toward this goal, but if you're doing a presentation for the first time notes may keep you from feeling too anxious. Notes are also very useful if you are running a day-long programme and want to be sure to stay on target regarding both content and timing. So notes are not necessarily a bad thing. But sometimes we don't use them well.

### Notes for a short presentation

There are a wide variety of ways to produce and use notes for short presentations.

### *Slide printout*

Many people like to print out their slides so that they can keep an eye on where their presentation is going. It works well to print three, four, or six slides to a page, and then to highlight parts of each slide for yourself. You can also write reminders in the margins if that helps you. Remember, though, that the more you write, the harder it will be for you to read. You want to avoid trying to decipher your own handwriting while you're presenting! I suggest that you simply note some key words that you can recognise at a glance, and trust yourself to fill in the rest.

## Keyword list

When I have to deliver a short presentation or a speech, I usually write out what I want to say, and then reduce each paragraph to a sentence expressing its main point. I then reduce this list of sentences to a list of words that remind me of each main point. I write these down or print them out in bold capitals on a piece of paper, so that when I begin my talk I have a clear list of words to guide me through it. For me, seeing a whole lot of words on a page of notes makes me more nervous, not less nervous, because the excitement of presenting makes it hard for me to read! I have also at times reduced these keywords to symbols, so that I have a series of pictures to help me along. An added benefit of this approach is that only I can understand the notes, and anyone looking at them can't predict what I'm going to say!

## Index cards

Index cards are extremely versatile tools for presenters. You can use small ones and write down one main point per card, or bigger ones that can include your main point and its sub-points as well. If you prefer to type, you can print your notes, cut them out, and paste them on the index cards. Remember to use a large font so that they are nice and easy to read when you need to refer to them. I like index cards because I find it relaxing to get through a point and then put the index card away. They can also help with timing. If you put your start time on the first card, then write on each card the ideal time for you to be starting on that topic, you can either speed up or slow down as you need to.

Because they are stiff, they hold up better than regular paper, and make less noise as well. I saw a wonderful conference presenter use them in a very creative way that took advantage of their sturdy nature. She was using 4x6 cards, and had punched a hole in the top left corner of each. She put a binder ring through the holes, and hung the binder ring around her finger. In this way, the index cards never got out of order and she didn't have to worry about putting them down or misplacing them. She could move around the stage at will, knowing that her cards were in the right order and that it wouldn't take but a moment to refer to them if she needed to. They didn't distract her, and they didn't distract us.

### Myth Buster

It is distracting to the audience if I hold my notes in my hands.

Actually, it can be more distracting if you have to keep returning to a podium or table to consult your notes. If you have made clear, easy-to-read notes for yourself, referring to them doesn't take long and doesn't interrupt the flow of your talk.

## Notes for a long presentation

Those of you who present for hours on end — perhaps because you are trainers, or because you are tasked with delivering huge end-of-year status reports and such — will no doubt be using some sort of note system already. If your notes are copious, do consider the advantages of whittling them down to key words and concepts so that you don't struggle with reading them, and also so that you keep your presentation fresh and engaging.

### Danger Zone

Relying on notes can hold you back from trusting yourself. Watch out for using notes rather than your brain, especially when you are growing used to a presentation.

## Full-day presentation aids

When you are required to speak or facilitate for the best part of a day, perhaps you'll need a combination of visual aids for yourself. Slides may be enough to get you through, but keeping to a schedule of content and activities is also really important. It can help a lot to have a printout of your slides so that you remember what's coming up and don't get ahead of yourself. I also recommend printing out a timetable for yourself that shows you what you want to be doing and when. For example:

9:00 Welcome and self-introduction

9:15 Group discussion on pros and cons of current software, use flipcharts

9:25 Group leaders provide feedback to rest of group

9:35 Introduction to new software package with reference to feedback

Etc.

## Star Tips for making sure your visual aids work for you

1. Make your message clearer and more memorable with visual aids.

2. Practice ensures that you will be able to survive without your slides.

3. Don't become a slave to your slides; be their master.

4. Corporate templates encourage consistency, but can also reduce creativity and make your presentation too predictable.

5. Grab your audience's attention and encourage engagement by memorising your agenda and delivering it in an interesting fashion.

6. Leave your listeners with a striking image, or return to a question you asked at the opening.

7. Include a call to action in your closing, to capitalise on the impact of your presentation.

8. Limit animation and colour in your slides as they can detract from your message, rather than solidify it.

9. Rather than letting your listeners read your handouts during your presentation, let them know that they can pick up copies on their way out.

10. Keep your slides simple, and layer your handouts with important, value-adding information that doesn't have a place in your presentation.

11. Consider using flipcharts and/or whiteboards as they can be very effective as a tool for teaching or maintaining interest, even if you have slides as well.

12. Use a remote control as it will allow you to move freely during a presentation.

13. Use notes in an efficient manner that won't interrupt your flow while you're presenting.

# TECHNICAL PRESENTATION CHALLENGES

*"Technology... is a queer thing. It brings you great gifts with one hand, and it stabs you in the back with the other."*

C.P. Snow

## How technical presentations are different... and the same

People who are required to deliver data-heavy, technical presentations understandably roll their eyes when people say things like "Use no more than six bullets per slide, and no more than six words per bullet." These presenters deliver numbers, show charts and diagrams, and discuss scientific processes or complicated economic arrangements. They often exist in a world beyond bullet points.

Nonetheless, the importance of clarity and simplicity remains paramount for technical people too. They just have to go about it differently.

## Charts and graphs

I was listening to a presentation that reported the results of a survey of a sector of the telecommunications industry. Early on in the presentation, the speaker showed a slide that included a bar chart, a graph, some text, and a pie chart. While he talked, I realised I couldn't follow him for several reasons:

- The legends under each chart were so small I couldn't read them, so I had no idea what each colour meant.

- The title for the Y-axis had been written sideways along the axis, and was too difficult to read.

- I could make out the words of the text, but it was frustrating because I didn't know whether to read them or listen to the presenter.

- My eyes like pie charts, so I ended up looking at that part of the slide, no matter what he was saying.

If, for some strange reason, you are convinced it is absolutely necessary to crush three charts and a small paragraph of text onto one slide, you have two choices. Either you can put it all up and act as a guide for your audience: "I'd like to draw your attention to the bar chart on the top left corner of the slide. It represents what happened to the sales of the top five companies last year." You'll need to be this clear for each part of the slide you are discussing; for example, "Now please take a look at this graph on the right." Remember that your listeners will be curious about the whole slide, so if you don't talk about each element of it, they will wonder what they've just missed. They will also wonder what it was doing there in the first place.

Your other (and in my mind, better) option is to build the slide. Bring up an empty slide with just the title at the top, and give your listeners an idea of what you are about to show them. Animate the slide so that your first chart appears when you click. Your listeners won't be distracted by anything else, and you will be able to speak about the chart without worrying that they aren't following. Once you're finished with that explanation, click again so that the next chart comes up. If you do this very clearly, you won't need to put up a paragraph of text at all.

**Fast Fact**

Listeners look at what they want to look at on your slides, not what you imagine they'll look at, or hope they'll look at.

## Divide and conquer

Your best option, in my opinion, is to have the charts on different slides. This feels like it will make your presentation a lot longer, but only if you consider your slides, rather than your message, to be your presentation. The length of a presentation is not determined by the number of slides, but by the ease and clarity with which you can deliver them. If you put three charts on one slide, they will be small and difficult to interpret for the listener. The job of explaining them will become more difficult as a result. If you give each chart its own slide, it won't challenge the listener's attention so much, and you as a presenter will have an easier time indicating the most important information on the chart. It won't take more time than having all the charts on one slide, and will often take less time.

It can be effective to put two charts or graphs on one slide in order to show how a situation has changed over time, but if you do so, be sure to bring up one chart and then the other. Putting them both up at once will have your listeners looking from one to the other, back and forth, trying to figure out the change for themselves, instead of letting you guide them through it.

## Charts have feelings too

You may recall that in Chapter 4 we discussed how often presenters say, "I have trouble presenting because my material is so dry." This is especially true of presenters who deal with technical content. However, there is always a way to enliven content. Vocal emphasis is one. Emotional words are another.

If, for example, you have a series of half a dozen charts to deliver, think about giving each of them a feeling or an image that represents their significance. You can use language like this to keep your listeners engaged, and to keep your own energy up as you deliver the information:

> *"I really love this graph because it shows just how right we were about the market."*

> *"I can't tell you how much I hate the next chart. But I have to show it to you because it will give you an idea of just how tricky things are in the industry right now."*

> *"It's so cool how this chart looks exactly like the Manhattan skyline. And just like Manhattan, it shows us a wide range of behaviour."*

> *"A lot of people wouldn't show you this chart, but I'm going to, because I'm convinced that it holds the seeds of a really good opportunity for us."*

Can you see how this language will hook a listener's curiosity? Not only that, it will impress any listener who is accustomed to dozing through the usual fare of "In the next slide, the chart shows..." and "Here's another graph showing..."

### Aha! Moment

As with any presentation, it will help me enormously to imagine myself in the listener's seat, asking how I would like to see each slide built and hear it described.

## Slides vs. take-home documents

Many times, when I talk to a client about how packed their slides are with data and how unnecessary it is to write everything they intend to say on them, they tell me they know it's an issue but that their slides also serve as a take-home document for their audience.

Think about the message that this sends your listener. Basically you are telling them, "I would rather make my slides really difficult for you to read, and my presentation much more complicated, than spend a bit of extra time producing a suitable slideshow and a suitable take-home document."

A presentation and a document are completely different animals. Trying to save a bit of time by turning them into one thing can really backfire. You're much better off developing the take-home document first, asking yourself the question, "What are all the details they might feel the need to know?" Once you've got all of that down in a logical structure, you can develop your presentation, choosing from that information as you ask yourself the main points you need to address during this presentation, and what would be the most helpful and interesting way to go about it.

Yes, this will take more time than you're used to devoting to a presentation. But if you do have the time and put in the effort, you'll become a much better presenter and, very importantly, a more valuable resource to your listeners.

If you absolutely don't have the time necessary to do so, make sure that you know how to explain your packed slides in a way that won't frustrate your listeners.

## Myth Buster

If my listeners can refer to a copy of my slides as I talk, they will understand me better.

In fact, when you give them a copy of your slides, they may read ahead and know what your main points are before you get to them. What's more, they will interpret them in their own way, rather than in the way you have planned. And some of them may tune you out altogether.

## Star Tips for enhancing the clarity of your technical presentations

1. Keep your delivery clear and simple when conducting technical presentations.

2. Don't let the number of slides dictate the length of your presentation; what's important is the ease with which you deliver them.

3. Avoid putting lots of charts on one slide. This makes it difficult for the listener to interpret and you to explain.

4. If you have lots of similar charts to deliver, consider giving each of them a feeling or an image that represents their significance.

5. Don't make your slides and take-home document one and the same. Doing so will reduce the effectiveness of both.

# MANAGING THE ENVIRONMENT

*"Character can dominate conditions. Will creates circumstances and environment."*

Anne Besant

## Arranging the furniture

 **Fast Fact**

If we don't take steps to manage the environment in which we are making our presentation, the environment will manage us.

### Room layout

Sometimes you'll be asked how you would like the room to be set up, particularly if your presentation has a training element to it. For a simple meeting, you'll be in someone's office or conference room, but for a larger group and a longer presentation, you might get a training room, or you might have booked space in a hotel. Unless you make your requirements for the layout clear, chances are you'll arrive to find things left as they were the last time the room was used. In the case of a hotel space, you might find tables in a U-shape with the projector table in the opening, leaving absolutely no space for approaching your listeners.

Here are your most common options:

### *U-shape*

This is a very helpful arrangement to choose when presenting to a small group of around 10 to 15 people, where you want to be able to interact with them. When you choose this shape, it's a good idea to tell the people who will be arranging the tables and chairs whether you want it to be a wide U (Illustration 9.1.1) or a narrow U (Illustration 9.1.2). Do you want there to be plenty of room in the middle of the U for you to walk around in? Or do you want the participants to be closer to each other, to promote discussion among them, but still leaving you enough space to get close to them? It can help to draw a picture of your desired arrangement for the organiser.

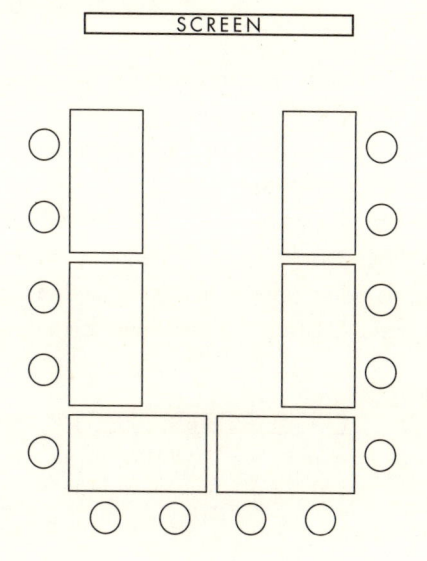

*Illustration 9.1.1 Wide U-Shape Arrangement*

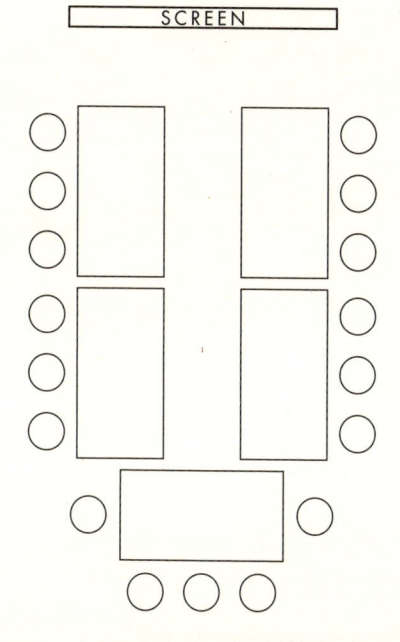

*Illustration 9.1.2 Narrow U-Shape Arrangement*

## Cluster seating

If your presentation includes a component of group discussion or other activity, cluster seating (see Illustration 9.2) is for you. This is best done at round tables, but can also be done at square or rectangular tables if that's all that's available. Not only does this arrangement promote interaction among the participants, but it also gives you plenty of opportunity to move among the tables. Round tables also tend to have more surface area than rectangular tables, so participants don't feel crowded together and there's enough space for them to take notes and have some drinks and snacks as well, if you wish.

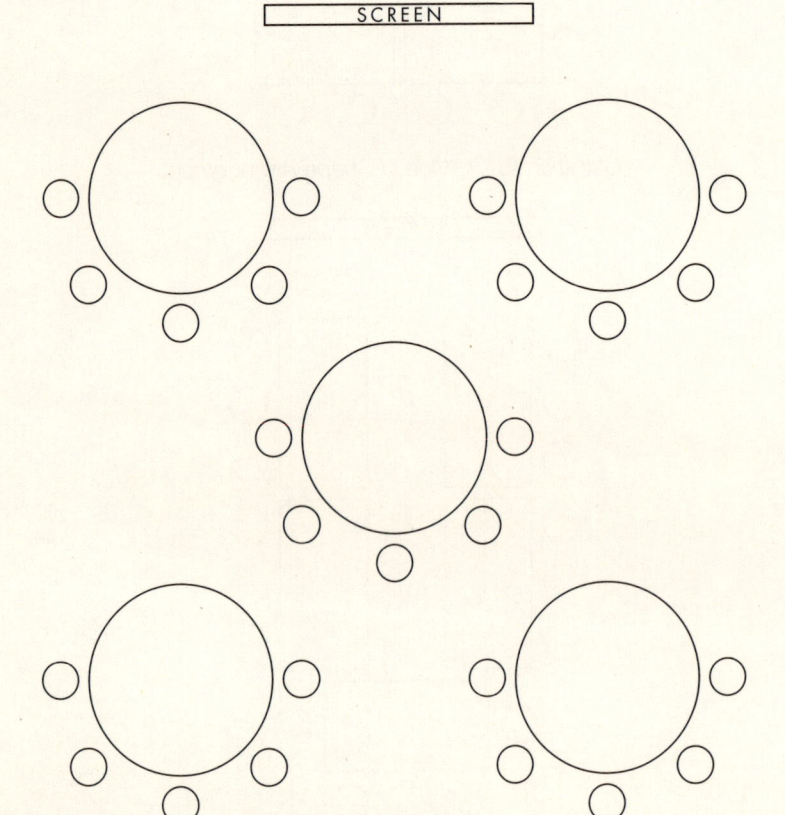

*Illustration 9.2*

## Table-less seating

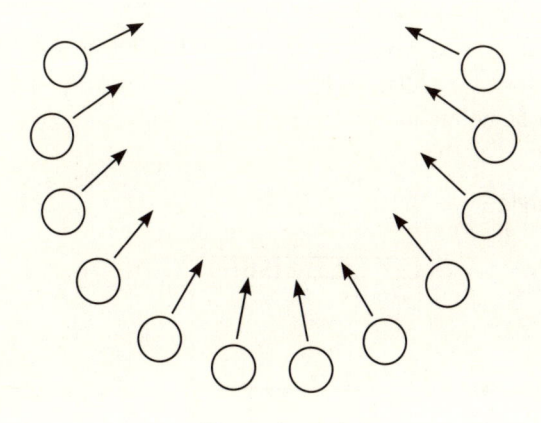

*Illustration 9.3.1*

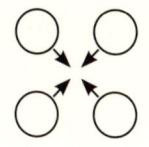 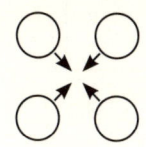

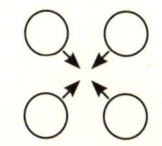

*Illustration 9.3.2*

This choice is less common, but if discussion is a high priority for you, do consider getting rid of tables and encouraging people to sit closely and interact more freely. This arrangement has the added advantage of ease of movement. You can start with the chairs in a big U (Illustration 9.3.1), and then ask people to take their chairs and form smaller groups (Illustration 9.3.2). If you want everyone standing for an activity, you can ask them to move the chairs all the way back to the wall to make space in the middle of the room.

### Classroom style

*Illustration 9.4*

I put this one last for a reason. It's my least favourite, and probably most people's least favourite. Who wants to be reminded of school? Who wants to look at the backs of so many heads? This is the least dynamic way to seat people for a presentation, but a lot of seminar organisers still arrange the room this way. Make sure you're clear about not wanting this layout if it would hurt your presentation success.

## Doing it yourself

When I arrive early in a meeting room, I think hard about where I want the people I'm meeting to be sitting, and about whether I will sit or stand. I always arrive early for training sessions, because training rooms are almost invariably set up in ways that limit my movement. In one location, the tables and chairs were exactly as I wanted them, but the wires for setting up my laptop and connecting it to the projector were arranged on a large podium so that I would have had to stand behind the podium to see the laptop screen. I changed things around so that I could come in front of the podium and move around the room, with easy access to my laptop.

We do this not just to make ourselves comfortable, but to be sure we have done as much as we can to develop an environment conducive to learning for our listeners, or the right atmosphere for discussion.

Other things you can do to develop an appropriate atmosphere for your presentation include:

- Opening or closing the curtains or blinds.
- Experimenting with the lighting.
- Removing some chairs to make the room feel less crowded for the listeners.
- Pushing chairs away from your laptop table so that you can move around it easily.
- Shifting an awkwardly placed table (often with the projector on it) so that you can approach your listeners.
- Opening a window to allow for fresh air.

## Arranging your mind

When you are taking such measures to improve the space, you are also beginning to make the space your own, even if you are in the meeting room of a potential client. In your mind, you are taking possession of the space. Of course this doesn't mean that you will actually behave as if you're on your own turf, but you will feel much more confident after arranging it to suit yourself.

When I rearrange things in a room before a presentation, I like to start thinking of the space as my own living room. This means that when people are listening to me, I don't approach them with an attitude that says "Thank you so much for having me here. I hope you like my presentation and I hope you agree with me," but rather "Welcome to this exchange of information. I'm very comfortable here, and I'm glad to be able to share my thoughts with you."

## Time killers

If your presentation set-up tends to take a long time and people might come early to the meeting, it's a nice idea to place product samples, flyers, books, or whatever is relevant to your subject on a table by the door or on individual seats, so that the early birds will have something to do while they wait. Such things can also lead to conversations that will help make you feel a bit closer to the audience even before you start. If your product samples are very interesting, however, you might want to get them back before you start presenting so that you have everyone's attention. You can give people an opportunity to investigate them again after your talk.

## Musical accompaniment

In a situation where you have invited people to come to a location to hear you speak — for example, if you are giving a product presentation in a hotel — it can be very nice to have music playing as they trickle into the venue. Hotel spaces can be quite anonymous, so you can give the space a bit of atmosphere by choosing the right music. It's not wise to choose something too fast or loud. Something too slow and soothing is also dangerous. Music that is gently upbeat will encourage people to feel welcome and will make them feel less awkward than they would be walking into a quiet room. People are often more willing to make conversation with each other when there is music to cover their voices.

## Let the walls speak for you

Rented presentation spaces, like hotels or training facilities, are perfect for putting up posters, laminated newspaper articles, and other information relevant to you or your talk. You can put your stamp on the surroundings, and participants can learn a bit more about you before and after your talk. Again, this can lead to some interesting conversations with you, and about you, before you've even turned on your laptop or positioned your flipchart.

## Meet and greet

Nothing brightens up a neutral room like a smile. Even if you are setting up when people arrive at the meeting, leave what you are doing, smile, shake the hand of the person who has arrived if that is normal for the culture, introduce yourself and welcome them. If you've put up posters or laid out samples, invite them to have a look. You will have warmed the environment in the room in this way, and when you are delivering your presentation you are likely to get a friendly look from them when your eyes meet.

If you are presenting to a client in their space, and the group is already assembled when you arrive, don't let concerns about time make you rush through your introductions. Greet each person in turn, telling those you've already met that it's good to see them again, and those you haven't met how glad you are to meet them. Having done this, you will feel more comfortable during your preparations, and can use the time to make some casual conversation as well. You might learn a few things that will help during your presentation!

### Myth Buster

If I arrive at a meeting last, I can't arrange the room to suit me.

Wrong! Even if you arrive at the meeting last, you can take a minute to move things around a bit in the space you plan to use. If you are more comfortable it will show, and this will make your listeners comfortable too. Few things are more distracting than a presenter who has to keep walking around a random chair or stepping over an unnecessary wire.

## Some like it hot... and others don't

Part of being attentive to your audience during a presentation is developing a feeling not just for their intellectual interest (or disinterest) in what you are saying and for their feelings about what you are saying, but also for their physical comfort. If you are cold before you begin speaking, it might not just be your nerves. The room may well be cold, and it's worth asking your listeners if they are comfortable. Do the same if you feel hot, or if you see people reacting to the room's temperature as they walk in. It's best to get the temperature sorted out before you start, as it can be distracting to a listener to feel chilly or sweaty, and I certainly find it distracting as a speaker to see my listeners shivering or fanning themselves.

If the room felt comfortable at the beginning of your talk, adding bodies and closing the door may cause it to heat up. If your presentation is quite long and you notice that people seem uncomfortable, do take a moment to enquire if they are hot or cold, and take the initiative to figure out how to adjust the temperature for them. They will certainly thank you for it, and are likely to listen to you with renewed interest when you resume speaking.

## Bang, bang! You're dead

Those of us who live in rapidly developing cities are very familiar with having to speak over pile drivers and jackhammers. If the construction is in the same building as your meeting or event, it sometimes works well to ask the builders if they'd be kind enough to take a break while you're delivering your presentation. Sometimes it doesn't work, however, and it's certainly not possible if the construction is across the street. In such cases, you have several options:

- If possible, arrange for a microphone.
- Rearrange the room so that you have your listeners in a tight semicircle with you standing quite close to them.
- If you are speaking at a small meeting, suggest that you continue to deliver your presentation in the room but adjourn to a quieter place

afterwards, perhaps a coffee shop in another building, for questions and further discussion. Presenters must be willing to shout sometimes, if necessary, but it's best not to expect listeners to do so as well.

If the noise is coming from voices or music at a vigorous meeting or event in the adjoining room, it's best to go next door and politely ask for their understanding in lowering their volume a bit. If they won't, or can't, then you can make the changes suggested above, or ask if there is another room available a bit further away. You'll have to set up again, but the move can actually add energy to your presentation, and you will have a common sense of purpose with your listeners: to hear and be heard.

## It's never too late to make changes

It's obviously best to arrive early enough at a meeting or speaking engagement to assess the environment and make adjustments that will suit your goals, but if for some reason you arrive just on time, it's not necessarily a problem to make some changes to the room. If you will be speaking and discussing for an hour, what's five minutes spent increasing the benefits of that hour? Naturally you'll want to ask permission of the person in charge of the meeting, but it would be very unusual for them to deny you a few minutes of 'environment enhancement'. Try it. And if they say no, it's okay. At least you tried.

### Aha! Moment

I don't have to adjust completely to the way a meeting room is set up, even if I am presenting in a client's office. I can make changes to improve the meeting environment, both for them and for me.

## Time management

If you're anything like me, when you're experiencing the adrenalin rush of presenting, you have trouble gauging how much time has passed. When I'm particularly excited, I sometimes look at my watch because I know I'm supposed to check on the time, but it makes absolutely no sense to me. Because of this, I benefit greatly (and so do my listeners!) if there's someone else keeping time during my talk. I ask them to hold up cards that show me that I have 20 minutes left, then 10 minutes, then 5 minutes. This keeps me calm, and as a result I can manage my material in the best way possible.

Obviously this technique works very effectively in large groups, such as at conferences. In meetings, you have to be able to manage time yourself.

I've seen quite a lot of presenters disregard time completely, particularly in sales presentations. Even when the buyer or manager or even CEO they are talking to asks them to finish in the next five minutes because of an upcoming appointment, the presenter merely carries on. Many of them don't even look at their watches, so how are they supposed to know how much time is passing?

Don't jeopardise your relationship with someone by not showing enough respect for their schedule. If there is a clock in the room that is visible from where you are presenting, keep an eye on it. Otherwise, take off your watch and put it next to your laptop so you can look at it frequently. Some people like to use their mobile phone as a clock, but since this often must be picked up or at least must have buttons pressed to check the time, it is more of a distraction than an aid. I'd get a watch. And if trying to read the long hand and the short hand don't work for you under stress, as they don't for me, get a digital one!

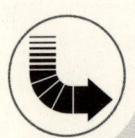 **Fast Fact**

Some remote controls allow you to set a timer that will show you how much time you have remaining as you conduct your presentation.

## Star Tips for creating the right speaking environment

1. Take steps to manage the environment. If you don't, the environment will manage you.

2. Adjust the environment not just to make yourself comfortable, but also to be sure it is conducive to learning and discussion.

3. It's nice to give the early birds something to do or read while they are waiting for you to begin.

4. Playing gently upbeat music can encourage people to feel welcome, and will make them feel less awkward about arriving in a quiet room.

5. Use the walls of rented presentation spaces to put up information relevant to your talk.

6. Nothing brightens up a room like a happy face.

7. Develop a feeling not only for your listeners' intellectual interest and engagement during your talk, but also for their physical comfort.

8. Even if you arrive at your presentation venue right at the appointed time, it's not necessarily a problem to make some changes to the room before you begin.

9. Don't jeopardise your relationship with someone by not showing enough respect for their schedule.

# TROUBLESHOOTING

*"Smooth seas do not make skillful sailors."*

African Proverb

## It depends on how you see it

Trouble for one person is another person's opportunity. I remember, early on in my speaking career, being amazed by a colleague who said he actually looked forward to something going wrong, like the projector bulb going out, so that he would have the chance to really show his mettle. In order to see unexpected circumstances as opportunities to distinguish yourself from other presenters, you have to have the confidence that you know your content and the situation well enough to adapt to new conditions on the spot.

A lot of this confidence will come from practising what we discussed in previous chapters: knowing your audience, managing your anxiety, practicing your presentation without your slides, and making sure the environment suits you and your listeners before you start. But even when you've worked on these elements, things can still take a strange turn.

Let's take a look at what you can do when even these efforts aren't quite enough. And then let's look at everyone's biggest worry — difficult questions.

## What to do if...

### 1. Your presentation is pitched at the wrong level

It's ideal to really know the audience you're speaking to, so that you choose your vocabulary and your approach for maximum impact. But a few things can sometimes get in the way. You might be asked to give your presentation at the last minute, so that all you can do is get the information together. Or you might be asked by a colleague to stand in for him or her, in which case you're not even delivering your own material.

In such situations, remember:

- You may not have time to get online or read the trade journals or do what you need to do to know the audience, but you can still make a phone call. Even if you do it literally on your way to the meeting, it is worth calling up the person responsible to ask a few questions. Something as simple as the age range of the listeners will be helpful, as this will let you decide which references or jokes will be well received. Ask as many things as you can think of. By the time you arrive you will no longer be in fear of the unknown, and you will have started formulating your approach.

- If you realise partway through your talk that your listeners have a much less advanced understanding of your topic than you had assumed, or had been led to believe, you need to acknowledge this. Don't just barrel on, as you will alienate them. If your goal at the outset had been to convince them of something, take a moment to shift and have your goal be to educate them. In this way you will lay the groundwork for convincing them in a follow-up meeting. Not laying this groundwork, trying to force action before your listeners are qualified to judge, will hurt you in the end.

- If, on the other hand, you discover, after some very sophisticated questions, that your presentation is too basic for your audience, my suggestion is to lean on your main objective, which is no doubt clearly laid out in your conclusion or call to action. Acknowledge to your listeners that you recognise that they are savvy on the subject, and jump to the end so that you can drive home your main point and spend the rest of the time allotted in discussion. Tell them that you are very interested not only in their questions but also in their own thoughts on the subject, since they are clearly knowledgeable. Turn your presentation into a real sharing of information.

 **Aha! Moment**

Even a last-minute effort to adapt to my audience can have an impact on my success.

## 2. You haven't practised without your slides, and they don't work

Above everything else in this situation, TRUST YOURSELF. The issue is not that you can't do the presentation without the slides. You can. The issue is that *you imagine* that you can't do the presentation without your slides. Remember how to calm yourself on the spot:

- Take a deep breath.

- Remember that everyone in the room would hate to be in your position.

- Smile.

- Tell everyone it's not a problem (and don't allow yourself to think it is).

- Check that the flipchart has paper and that the markers work.

- Ask them to give you a short moment to think about how you will approach the presentation without the slides.

- Think quietly, staying positive, remembering your main objective and important points.

- Tell them you'll do your very best, and will forward the slides to anyone who wants them after you get back to the office.

- Smile again.

- Do your best.

- Encourage discussion.

 **Aha! Moment**

It's a good idea always to have a printout of my slides with me, so that in a situation like this I can refer to them easily.

## Handling difficult questions

Even people who are comfortable with their research and delivery often dread the question and answer period. They experience a fearful anticipation of questions they can't answer, or questions they'd rather avoid. This sense of nervousness naturally affects their ability to answer any question to best effect.

**Fast Fact**

Remember, the brain has trouble functioning smoothly under stress.

### Practice makes perfect

Before we discuss ways of managing questions on the spot, it's important to point out how much of this stress can be avoided with one simple, powerful activity: role-playing. You may already practice your presentation before delivering it — or you may be about to start doing so after reading this book — but do you practice answering questions? Very few people do. If you become one of them, you'll be doing yourself an enormous favour.

Perhaps you're saying to yourself that it would be too much of an imposition on a colleague to ask them to take the time to do this Q&A role-playing with you, but in fact you would almost certainly be doing them a service as well. If you approach someone who is in a similar position to yours, and who has to give presentations as well, then it will be good practice for both of you, and you can pick each other's brains for information and techniques. Take turns playing the role of presenter and the role of audience, and ask each other the most difficult questions you can think of. Then, critique each other's answers, and offer helpful suggestions. If there are situations where neither of you knows what to say, take it to a higher level. Any manager who sees his or her staff making this sort of effort is bound to be impressed, and will share relevant experience as well.

Everyone gains new information, and you can go into your presentation knowing that you are not alone; you have the knowledge and support of your department and your organisation behind you.

What this will mean is that when a question comes up that you have already practised, you will be able to plug in to your answer right away, feeling and looking more confident. It also allows you to begin your answer with phrases like, "I'm glad you asked, as I was just discussing this with colleagues yesterday," showing how topical their question is. They'll love it.

Now let's take a look at some ways of managing questions you haven't prepared for. (Shame on you!)

### Sensitive questions

As with most difficult questions, you won't be surprised to hear that there isn't one way to deal with them. Unlike the police, we can't simply say, "We assure you that we are following all possible lines of enquiry." You will have to decide whether you must say nothing, or whether you can say something, or if it's safe to trust your audience completely. Again, it is best to get guidance from the leadership of your organisation in order to be sure you are doing the right thing. But if caught unawares by a question on something you hoped wasn't public knowledge, here are some approaches you can use.

| | |
|---|---|
| **Pass the buck:** | "Actually, I'm not authorised to talk about that. If you like, I can put you in touch with someone who is." Remember you must follow through with this as soon as possible after your presentation. |
| **Offer some crumbs:** | "I'm sure you know that is a delicate subject, and I don't anticipate being able to give you a complete answer for another week (or fortnight, or month) or so. However, what I can tell you is…" |

Using this approach, you will appear willing and helpful, even if you are still very limited in what you can say.

**Dig deeper and start a conversation:** "I'm interested as to why you asked this question. Do you work in an area that will be affected by my answer?" This will give you time to learn more about the person who asked the question, and to think of a way to offer something that is helpful to them without giving everything away.

**Empathise, and ask for empathy in return:** "I can absolutely understand why this information is important to you, and I respect that you asked the question. I think you can probably understand why I don't feel I can give you that information right now. Perhaps you could give me your contacts, and I can let you know when the public can have access to it." While the person who asked the question may feel that you are being cagey, they will be surprised that you are showing a willingness to stay in touch.

## Questions beyond your expertise

No doubt you've already read or heard that it's better to say that you don't know something than to get tangled up in a patchy answer. Well, I'm here to say it again. It is. However, it's not usually fine simply to say, "I don't know." Follow it up with something helpful:

- "I don't know much about that side of things, but I'd be happy to call you this afternoon with an answer/e-mail you this afternoon with the relevant data."

- "Actually, I'm quite new in this department, so if you don't mind, I'd rather put you in touch with my senior colleague to make sure you get

the best answer possible to your very good question. Will you be free
to take a call later today, or shall I have her e-mail you?"

- "Thanks for that question. I haven't ever looked at things that way.
Would you mind giving me the time to think about it for a while and
I'll get in touch? You gave me your card, didn't you?"

 **Myth Buster**

Questions are terrible things. They are out to get us
and make us look foolish.

Wrong! The great thing about questions you can't
answer is, every single one will lead you to increase
your knowledge. See them as gifts.

### Questions that become lectures or diatribes

While most people listening to presentations are there to increase or test
their knowledge, some people attend in order to prove their knowledge.
Sometimes they do this by interrupting you, sometimes by waiting until
the end to put you to the test. I have seen presenters who become very
defensive when this happens, and it's not the best approach. Being
defensive not only plays into the hands of the person who is testing you,
but also diminishes your status in the eyes of the other listeners.

### The Interrupter

When someone begins by asking a question but carries on talking about
their view of things in the middle of your presentation, it works well to
say something like, "You've asked a great question and I'm sure we'd all
like to discuss it, but I'd like to get through my main points, which may
address a few of your issues. If you are unsatisfied at the end, I'll be very
happy to open the discussion again." They might agree. They also might
not. If they keep talking, you probably need to be more assertive: "Thank
you. At this point I'd like to ask the rest of the listeners if they'd like me

to stop my presentation altogether to discuss your question, or if they would prefer to listen to what I have to present and keep the discussion until the end." It's possible that what your interrupting listener is asking is foremost in everyone's mind, and they will in fact say they want the discussion to continue. However, it is more likely that they will ask you to continue with what you had planned. In this way it is the other listeners, not you, who have requested the interrupter to wait.

## The Expert

If you have finished your presentation and someone takes the Q&A period as an opportunity to put forward their own views on the subject you have been addressing, you can't ask them to wait. You will have to deal with it. There are several ways to do so.

First, be aware of the reaction of the other listeners. If you can tell that they are of the same opinion as the speaker, just accept that the group wants you to hear all of what he or she has to say. Remember, Q&A periods can educate you as much as they can the people asking questions. Anyone with a dissenting opinion or different information from yours can actually be very helpful to you, even if you find their tone aggressive. Try not to take their comments personally, and show your willingness to listen and to address their concerns.

If, on the other hand, you can tell that the other listeners are uncomfortable with the way the speaker is monopolising the Q&A time, here is some language you can use to improve the situation:

*"I'm sorry to interrupt you because your comments are really interesting, but I'm concerned about the time. Can you limit what you want to say to a question right now, so others can ask what they want to as well, and then we can return to what you were saying again? I'm happy to stay behind if you want to get into an in-depth discussion."*

*"I'm sorry to interrupt but in the interest of time I'm going to have to ask you if you have a question I can answer first. Once I have dealt with any questions from the whole group, then we can get back into this discussion with you."*

## Managing your thoughts

Sometimes we have the information necessary to answer a question in our heads, but we have trouble organising it on the spot. This can undermine our confidence as we find ourselves rambling, and this can also undermine our listeners' confidence in us. A great way to manage this problem is to practice three great ways of organising information.

### The rule of three

In this approach, you tell your listeners that there are three important things they need to know about the subject they have brought up. Don't worry if you don't have three things foremost in your mind right away. They will come. When you give your brain a task and let it do its work, it won't let you down. If you worry, you'll get in its way. So say, "There are three things you need to know about X. The first is..." While you are saying this, the first thing will come to mind. Your mind will not offer up something unrelated to the subject: it will come up with something appropriate. Then, while you are talking about the first thing, your mind will be coming up with the second thing. It remembers that you asked for three things, so it will look for three things. And while you are talking about the second, you will be coming up with the third, without having to try very hard.

A wonderful aspect of this approach is that it is not only helpful for you; it is very helpful for the listener as well. Listeners prefer organised information they don't have to sort through. Packaging it in groups of three is perfect. Also, chances are they will listen all the way to the end of your answer. If you just ramble, they might well tune out, but if you've said there are three things to remember, they'll wait until they've heard all three. Practice this during your pre-presentation role-plays. You'll be amazed!

## Past and present

This technique is a great way to put things into context. If a listener asks about something happening in your company, you can start by saying, "It used to be that we did things in a different way" and then describe how. Then you can say, "Today, however, we have innovated to an extent that we have a new approach," and then describe that. Again, you've given yourself a bit of time to think, and have added value to your answer. Make sure that in your first sentence you make clear that you are talking about the past, and then your listeners will stay engaged to hear about how things have changed.

## Two sides of the coin

This approach gives a real richness to your answer, even if you have been asked a 'yes' or 'no' question. Imagine you've been asked if a majority of consumers is interested in saving money rather than buying quality. If the answer is yes, you can simply say so. However, it is more interesting, and a better way to show your knowledge and experience, to instead say, "On the one hand, yes. Most consumers are tightening their belts at the moment. On the other hand, however, the consumers who still want to spend still want to spend a *lot*."

All three of these approaches give you the chance to very quickly take your knowledge and chunk it down into more manageable pieces, as well as to sound more clear and capable than one does when simply launching into an answer without a structure. Try them all, and make them a useful part of your repertoire. People will remember you for it.

## Avoid ending on a sour note

My recommendation to anyone who wants to make sure that things end in an upbeat fashion is this: Do not let the Q&A period be the last moment of your presentation. It makes much more sense to place a time for questions *before* your final comments and call to action.

Think about it. Sometimes there are no questions at all. Do you want to end on silence? Even a warm thank you after a dead Q&A session can be a very low-energy way to end what might have been a very good presentation. Sometimes, on the other hand, the Q&A period can be a tense one. Perhaps you've had some very challenging questions and have had to pass the buck more than once. Is this what you want them to remember above all? Unlikely.

Simply place your Q&A before you wrap up your thoughts, and you avoid giving your listeners control over the tone of the end of the event. Once you've dealt with all the questions, step forward and tell them you'd like to close with a reminder, or a question, or a story, or a picture. Use this as your springboard to your call to action, so that this is the last thing they will remember. If you've done it well, it will also be the first thing they do.

## Star Tips for managing unexpected or unwelcome events

1. Treat trouble as an opportunity to learn and flex your presentation muscles!

2. Knowing your audience, practising your presentation, and role playing your Q&A period will help you avoid many types of trouble.

3. Make an effort to find out a little about your audience; even just knowing their age range or their level of experience will guide your approach.

4. Be prepared to abandon your presentation and focus on discussion if you find your audience has a sophisticated understanding of your subject.

5. You can deliver your presentation sufficiently even if your slides malfunction. Trust yourself!

6. It's okay to say you don't know, as long as you can follow up with a way to get the desired information.

7. Using tools for managing your thoughts on the spot will lead to enormous benefits for both you and your listeners.

# INDEX

# ABOUT THE AUTHOR

Alison Lester was born in the United States and is now based in Singapore. She is an associate of ST Training Solutions and director of AJ Lester Communication Training. While she has a bachelor's degree in Chinese and French, and a master's degree in Chinese studies, and has worked as a government desk officer, financial editor, and freelance writer, she bases most of her professional approach on her experience as a speaker, corporate trainer, and comedian.

Travelling around the world leading presentation skills workshops in countries as diverse as the Czech Republic, China, France, and the United States has given Alison a broad perspective on what presentations work and what complicates matters when we get up to speak to each other. She is delighted to have the opportunity to set it all down in this book.

---

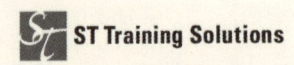 **ST Training Solutions**

## *Success Skills Series*

ST Training Solutions, based in Singapore, offers a wide range of popular, practical training programmes conducted by experienced, professional trainers. As CEO, Shirley Taylor takes a personal interest in working closely with trainers to ensure that each workshop is full of valuable tools, helpful guidelines and powerful action steps that will ensure a true learning experience for all participants.

Shirley Taylor is also host of a very popular annual conference called ASSAP — the Asian Summit for Secretaries and Admin Professionals — organised in April each year by ST Training Solutions.

Find out more about ST Training Solutions at www.shirleytaylortraining.com.